ESİN ÇELEBİ BAYRU

LOVE IS SOMETHING BEAUTIFUL

NEFES
history

ESİN ÇELEBİ BAYRU

Esin Çelebi, 22nd generation granddaughter of Hazrat Mevlânâ Celâleddîn-i Rûmî (Mawlana Jalaluddin Rumi), was born in Aleppo on April 2, 1949. She is a graduate of Istanbul Işık High School, having completed her primary, secondary and high school education there. Afterwards, she studied Arabic and Persian Philology at Istanbul University, Faculty of Literature.

Esin Çelebi has been serving as the vice-chairperson of the International Mevlânâ Foundation since its establishment in 1996. During this period, the Foundation has developed two key projects -among its other major initiatives- and worked with the Ministry of Culture and Tourism for submission of these works to UNESCO. As a result, UNESCO proclaimed "Semâ and the Mevlevî Music" as "an oral and intangible cultural heritage of humanity", declared 2007 to be the International Year of Mevlânâ, and accredited the Foundation.

Esin Çelebi also acts as a counselor to the Rumi Research and Implementation Center at Konya University. She is the editor of three published books, namely "Hz. Mevlânâ Okyanusundan" (From Hz. Mevlânâ's Ocean), featuring the conference and symposium proceedings of her father Celâleddin Bâkır Çelebi, "Yüzyıllar Boyu Mevlânâ ve Mevlevîlik Mevlânâ and Mevlevî Order Throughout Centuries" (bi-lingual Turkish - English book), written by scholars in the field for an in-depth coverage of the Mevlevî discipline, etiquette and rules of conduct (âdap and erkân), semâ, and semâ music, "Mevlânâ'dan Mevlâ'ya ulaşanlar" (Those Who Reach from Mevlânâ to Mawla), on the foreign Mevlevîs who live abroad. And she has various published articles and interviews in several periodicals. Esin Çelebi participates in local and international TV broadcasts as a speaker; she also gives public speeches at various local and international schools and universities. She continues her efforts to pass on Mevlânâ's universal thought and discipline, his exemplary lifestyle and the Mevlevî culture as a path of etiquette, correct behavior (âdap).

She received in May 2011 an honorary PhD from the Berkeley California Starr King School for The Ministry in the United States, in recognition for her works and contributions in the topic of "World Peace, Justice and Unity".

Esin Çelebi is married with two children.

Contents

Perspective really matters in life. Take, for instance, this window in my room: you may look at it, or look out of it. The former shows us a dirty pane of glass wetted by raindrops, true? But the latter reveals us the tomb of Hz. Mevlânâ, a beautiful view. Praise Allah.

Photograph 1: Esin Çelebi Bayru and Dilek Güldütuna.

Photograph 2: Esin Çelebi Bayru and Nefes Publishing staff.

ACKNOWLEDGEMENTS

Esin Çelebi Bayru

Every book has a background story, like this one.

Back in 2002, the first time I had participated in Selçuk University 10th National Mevlânâ Congress with a paper titled "My Father Celâleddin Bâkır Çelebi". My professors Emine Yeniterzi and Nuri Şimşekler had encouraged me a lot for that.

A few years ago, we were in a symposium in Izmir. As we went out during a break, at one point in our chat, I mentioned a memory, and Professor Mehmet Demirci asked: "Çelebi, I wonder if you are writing these..." I said, "Honestly, I am a bit lazy when it comes to writing. Not to mention the fast pace of my life. Time flies, and there's no time to write."

Professor said: "Cemâlnur, please designate one of your students. These memories must be written. This is oral history and these anecdotes need to be recorded."

It was in another symposium that I also heard similar comments from Professor Cihan Okuyucu. I thought I should say "*Eyvallah!*", which means "*All right, agreed!*" This is how I embarked upon the adventure of writing this book.

First, I would like to give my heartfelt thanks to my professors Emine Yeniterzi, Nuri Şimşekler, also Cemâlnur *Hanım,* Professor Cihan Okuyucu, and Professor Mehmet Demirci, who inspired the idea of writing this book.

Dilek Güldütuna, with her calmness, was of great help; she worked selflessly. Perhaps the most important of all was that we could record interviews with my mother. This is a major achievement, considering that my mother had never allowed this before.

Belgin Batum, Kerim Güç... You contributed a lot.

Dear Sertap Yar and Can Aydoğmuş, your studies formed the foundation of this book.

I would like to express my gratitudes to all who shaped me into who I am today and a heartfelt thanks to all who contributed to this book. May you give me your blessings for everything you provided.

FOREWORD

Dilek Güldütuna

This book is a series of conversations with Esin Çelebi Bayru, 22nd generation granddaughter of Hz. Mevlânâ Celâleddîn-i Rûmî (Mawlana Jalaluddin Rumi). Mrs. Bayru's mother Güzîde Çelebi also participated in some of these conversations. Professor Mehmet Demirci prepared the primary basis of questions for the interviews, which took part mostly in fall 2017 and were completed within a year.

The idea of this book was born in a casual conversation that took place in a symposium gathering.

The memories of the Çelebi family are not merely the story of one of the oldest families in history; it is the history of a culture, an entire tradition. It is a living archive that sheds light on the rapid changes faced by the Sufi culture and Sufi way of life in Turkey, and in particular on the Mevlevî Order, one of the first Sufi orders to emerge in Islam. These valuable anecdotes had to be saved from loss; they needed to be obtained from a credible source and recorded so that they are turned into lasting texts for the benefit of people today.

The interview questions prepared by Professor Mehmet Demirci, as well as the initiative and support of Professor Cemâlnur Sargut formed the starting point of this work. Besides the questions and topics that spontaneously emerged in the course of the interviews, we made use of the records of the previous interviews performed by Sertap Yar and Can Aydoğmuş with Esin Çelebi Bayru.

This book intends to present the memoirs of Esin Çelebi Bayru in chronological order. Mrs. Bayru was born and raised in Aleppo. After spending her childhood years there, she moved to Istanbul, where she spent most of her adult life. At present, she is the vice-chairperson of the International Mevlânâ Foundation. Therefore, this book consists of three chapters: i) Aleppo and childhood years, ii) Istanbul years, a chapter that includes the family's sudden move, iii) establishment of the International Mevlânâ Foundation and its ongoing activities.

We wished to enrich the journey of the reader by supporting the narrative with pictures, hence by including various types of visuals in the book. These are mainly the photographs of the Çelebi family and other people mentioned in the book, the photos demonstrating the Foundation's activities, as well as a number of documents and pictures.

Also, the reader can find a glossary of terms at the end of this book, as the text had to include some terms specific to the Mevlevî and Turkish culture. These particular words are marked in the text in italics.

Although the primary concern was not writing a Mevlevî family history, we believe these interviews will shed light on an essential era from the perspective of the history of Sufism in Turkey and will provide insights into the contemporary form of activities and services of the Mevlevî Order, as well as the progress of the Mevlevî thought and culture throughout the Republican Era. Starting with his son Sultan Veled, Hz. Mevlânâ's lineage had the honor of conveying Mevlânâ's discipline and thought. The lineage played a central role in basing the Mevlevî Order on strong foundations and in disseminating Hz. Pîr's work to the masses. As an important signifier of Turkish culture, the Mevlevî tradition is regarded as one of the most effective agents in the evolution of Turkish culture and arts. As such, in this book, the reader will hopefully trace the evolution of the Mevlevî Order with its mission from the time of Hz. Mevlânâ till today, also the contemporary form taken by the Mevlevî activity after the abolishment of the Sufi orders with the foundation of the Turkish Republic.

Esin Çelebi, through her memoirs, shares with us her childhood and her first *semâ* education, her life in Istanbul and the relationships of her family with the distinguished names of that era, information about Atatürk's visits to the Dervish Lodge in Konya (known today as the Mevlânâ Museum), the endeavors of her father Celâleddin Bâkır Çelebi as the founder of the foundation, the general stance taken by the foundation since its establishment, the activities carried out for proper communication, correct understanding and conservation of Mevlânâ's thought and discipline, as well as information about the services continuing today. She relays the messages that Hz. Mevlânâ intended to give to humanity.

Esin Çelebi is the vice-chairperson of the International Mevlânâ Foundation, a key institution in conservation of the cultural heritage of Hz. Mevlânâ. She also acts as consultant to the Rumi Research and Implementation Center at Konya University. She is the editor of three published books, namely "From Hz. Mevlânâ's Ocean", featuring the conference and symposium proceedings of her father Celâleddin Bâkır Çelebi, "Mevlânâ and Mevlevî Order Throughout

Centuries", written by scholars in the field for an in-depth coverage of Mevlevî discipline, etiquette and rules of conduct (*âdap and erkân*), *semâ*, and *semâ* music, "Those Who Reach from Mevlânâ to Mawla", on the foreign Mevlevîs who live abroad. And she has various published articles and interviews in a number of periodicals.

To communicate the universal thought and discipline of Mevlânâ, his exemplary lifestyle and the Mevlevî culture as a path of spiritual courtesy *(edep)*, Esin Çelebi gives public speeches at local and international schools, as well as speaking in local and international TV broadcasts. She received in May 2011 an honorary PhD from the University of Berkeley California Starr King School for The Ministry in the United States, in recognition of her works and contributions in the topic of "World Peace, Justice and Unity". We hope that one day her writings will be compiled in a book and be published, thereby coming back to us. Those written works include numerous papers, articles, proceedings that were prepared as part of countless conferences on Hz. Mevlânâ and the Mevlevî Order organized both by the Foundation and various other institutions as part of the long-standing services of the Foundation and the family.

Information that we come across in various studies on the Mevlevî Order from the past to today is provided here in firsthand form, and in colloquial, easy to read language. Therefore, we hope that a wider audience can benefit from this book. I would like to thank first of all, my professor Cemâlnur Sargut, who made it possible for me to work on the preparation of this book, to Mrs. Esin Çelebi Bayru, with whom we worked together with pleasure, a lady who beautifully reflects Mevlevî grace and manners, to her mother

Mrs. Güzîde Çelebi, who is 91 as of today, who honored us with her participation in our interviews, and to all our friends who supported us.

November 2018
Frankfurt am Main

ALEPPO DAYS

Can you briefly tell us about your life story?

I was born on April 2, 1949, in Aleppo, Syria. I went to Istanbul Işık High School, where I completed my primary, secondary and high school education. Then I studied Arabic and Persian Philology at Istanbul University, Faculty of Literature.

I am married to Osman Bayru, a grandchild of *Osman Efendi-Sheikh of the Yenikapı Mevlevî House.* We have two daughters, Azra and Esra, two sons-in-law, Mehmet Kumcuoğlu and Ersev Demiröz, three grandchildren, Nil, Mina and Can Ata.

At present, I serve as the vice-chairperson of the International Mevlânâ Foundation, and also as a consultant to the Rumi Research and Implementation Center at Konya University.

I understand that you spent your childhood years in Aleppo.

Between Aleppo and Istanbul, indeed. My grandfather Mehmed Bâkır Çelebi had been appointed as the *Sheikh of the Aleppo Mevlevî House* before the enactment of the Law of Dervish Lodges (*Tekke and Zâviye Law*) that had ordered the abolishment of the Sufi centers in Turkey. My father Celâleddin Bâkır Çelebi was born there. I and three of my siblings were born there, while our youngest sibling was born when we came to Istanbul. At school age, I came to live with my maternal grandmother together with my brother Faruk Hemdem Çelebi. My father, mother, my paternal grandmother and grandfather are all Turkish, so our home was a Turkish speaking environment. Likewise, our children were raised, and grandchildren are being raised according to the Turkish tradition and culture. We refrain from imposing dos and don'ts on our children regarding the Mevlevî culture. We instead try to demonstrate living examples with our behavior. As our children observe the beauties of this culture, they appreciate it and automatically want to adopt and continue it.

Can you tell us about the environment in which you were raised?

I am the eldest of five siblings. Although my brother Faruk Hemdem Çelebi is 21 months younger than me, we regard him as the eldest in the spiritual sense. Besides him, I have three sisters.

Emel Çelebi Gürsoy, Neslipir Çelebi Sayar and Gevher Çelebi. All of us were raised in a very nice setting. My mother and father were cousins, and that turned out to be a great advantage for us. My father was raised in Aleppo and my mother in Istanbul. Although they had met once when they were children, they don't remember that encounter. Later, during a trip to visit his family in Istanbul, my father met my mother and fell in love at first sight; they were both in their 20s.

I am quite happy to say: "I was born to parents who are in love." Although my mother says, "Don't say that, I'm embarrassed", I get a sheer enjoyment from that. It was love at first sight, my parents got married, and we were surrounded by that love and respect at home, it always lasted.

My paternal grandmother was living with us. She was also the aunt of my mother. They were already close and got along very well. So, we were raised in a peaceful, happy, beautiful setting. This could indeed serve as an example to young people today. We also tried to raise our children in much the same way. Now they are passing it on to their children. Being raised in a peaceful family really has a big impact on how one lives and perceives life.

The German Orientalist Hellmut Ritter mentions about your paternal grandmother İzzet Hanım that she made Mevlevî clothes for a Mevlevî child who was learning semâ.

Yes, my grandmother offered great services. Consider that she and her sisters were raised in Aleppo, Syria in Ottoman times. At the time, her father Cherkes Mehmed *Bey* was called "Commandant of Extraordinary", which is a kind of Governor for Emergency State, a military governor.

Photograph 3: Cherkes Mehmed Bey and his children.

My maternal grandmother Nüzhet Hanım -also being the sister of my paternal grandmother- came to Istanbul after she married. My paternal grandmother stayed in Aleppo. Then she got married to my grandfather Mehmed Bâkır Çelebi. She married into a family with a life in a Mevlevî House (*Mevlevîhâne*) and adapted herself very well to a big family. My mother lived in the *harem* part of the Mevlevî House, together with her mother-in-law Kevser *Hanım*, Kevser *Hanım*'s mother-in-law Fatma *Hanım*, and two sisters-in-law Rukiye and Növber *Hanım* and her brother-in-law Şemsü'l-Vahid Çelebi. Because at the time, Mevlevî Houses in Turkey were closed due to the Law of Dervish Lodges. My grandfather's father, Abdülhalim *Chalabi* passed away; therefore, my grandfather took his family with him. My grandmother always spoke very highly of her life there.

I learned so much from my paternal grandmother. I had a lot of influence from her. When I was born, and once I was brought home from the hospital, she took me into her room and then carried me back to my mother regularly at the times of breast-feeding. My mother always says: "I gave birth to five children, but each time I was so comfortable and peaceful, I was pampered and coddled by your grandmother during these *lohusa* days."

My paternal and maternal grandmothers were sisters, so my parents were cousins. My maternal grandma was the eldest, and my paternal grandma was the second youngest among their siblings. My maternal grandma was a true Cherkes lady. She was commanding respect with her tall, majestic figure. There was a saying in the Old Istanbul: *vardakosta*... I guess this word migrated from Romaic. It means beautiful, nice and majestic at the same time. She was just like that, while inside, she had a soft heart. Paternal grandma was petite, but her obedient, milky air was in stark contrast with her strong-willed, amazingly powerful personality. I was raised and disciplined by both, and I took after both of them.

Yes, my paternal grandmother at a very young age married into a family at the Aleppo Mevlevî House, and therefore knew extensively about the Mevlevî Order and the discipline of Mevlevî Houses. We were raised by her, we learnt a lot from her.

Photograph 4: İzzet Hanım and Bâkır Çelebi.

My grandmother married a Chief Master, she undertook duties and responsibilities related to the life in a Mevlevî House, and she raised my father. These are all important because my grandfather Bâkır Çelebi passed away at a very young age. Coming from a military family, İzzet Hanım was a Turkish lady with a deep sense of loyalty to her country and culture, although she had a life abroad. While raising her children in the Mevlevî House, she also had them sent to French schools so that they acquire and combine scientific, material knowledge and spiritual wisdom through their education. Her children spoke very good French, Arabic and English -besides native Turkish-, and were familiar with Latin based languages.

In 1939, my grandfather came to Istanbul for the wedding of his niece, only to see that it was meant to be a one-way trip. On his way back, he wasn't let in as the Syrian Government claimed he worked in the annexation of Hatay. So, he went back to Istanbul to live with his aunt.

Meanwhile, my grandfather had brought presents from Beirut for his aunt and niece. He had even bought the wedding dress and participated in the wedding ceremony. I didn't have the chance to know that niece as she passed away at a young age, but today I am married to her son Osman Bayru. The wedding presents from my grandfather were in the later years given to me, and I then passed them on to my daughters at the time of their weddings as a keepsake from their grandmother.

I would like to emphasize this; my mother married her cousin; my father and my husband Osman Bey are the grandchildren of two siblings, but both are marriages of love. Our families didn't tell us to marry each other. We fell in love, just like my parents. We were very young at the time, therefore had a long period of engagement before getting married in 1972. May Allah bless us with a peaceful, healthy life.

Yes, love is something beautiful...

So says Hz. Mevlânâ: "All kinds of love are bridges to the divine love."

Photograph 5: Family photograph.

I tell this to young people: "When you are in love, it's the time you converse with Allah the most. Dear Allah, let me see my beloved, my dear Allah, I saw him, my dear Allah, if only he sends me a message, dear Allah he sent! if only he calls, oh he called!..." One keeps on talking to Allah, making wishes, thanking for wishes granted or whining about the ones not granted. For that matter, Hz. Mevlânâ says: "All kinds of love are bridges to the divine love."

You keep your grandfather Mehmed Bâkır Çelebi's ring. How did it reach you?

It's been handed to me by my grandfather Mehmed Bâkır Çelebi's wife, whom he had married after separation from my grandmother upon his forced return to Turkey that I've just mentioned. My grandmother stayed in the Mevlevî House with the children; my grandfather stayed in Turkey. He lived in Konya for a while, got married with Münîre Hanım and passed away soon after that. Years passed, we moved to Turkey, and one day, Münîre Hanım visited us. My grandmother was quite nice to her. She even said to us later: "Dear child, we had gotten divorced anyway, I stayed in Aleppo and raised our children there. At least she took care of your grandfather. I got nothing against her." Grandma was such a lovely, affectionate person indeed. May Allah bless her soul.

Later, when I wanted to give Münîre *Hanım* my wedding invitation, she gave me a ring as a present and said: "Your grandfather used to wear this. It was his grandfather's seal." So, Mehmed Bâkır Çelebi turned his grandfather's seal into a signet ring, and Münîre *Hanım* handed it to me. I am the fifth generation. I got very excited, and as soon as I came home, I wanted to pass it on to my father. When I said: "This was your father's ring, and your grandfather's seal. Although Münîre *Hanım* gave it to me, I believe this belongs to you rather than me", my father looked at the ring and said, "Dear daughter, this was given to you," and gave it back to me.

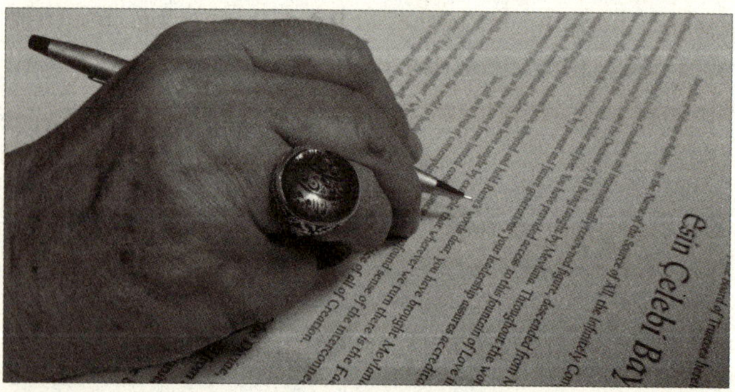

Photograph 6: Mehmed Bâkır Çelebi's ring.

I wear this with honor. It isn't exactly everyday jewelry for me; it is special. It has an onyx stone, on which there's an engraved inscription, reading "*Mevlânâ es-Seyyid eş-Şeyh el-Hâc Mehemmed (bin) bende-i Hâlik-i Hayy-ı dânâ 1199* (Mevlânâ the Syed Sheikh Hadji Mehemmed the slave of Allah the creator the one who's alive and the one who knows all, 1784-85)".

What was your grandmother's wedding present?

My grandmother İzzet Hanım passed away in 1971. It had been six months since she's gone when we got married in January 1972. She liked my husband Osman Bayru a lot. Having health problems during her last one year and thinking that she may not be able to see our wedding, she had gifted us her wristwatch beforehand.

Photograph 7: Esin Çelebi with her paternal grandmother İzzet Hanım.

Güzîde Çelebi: İzzet Hanım was an easy-going, accommodating person. We lived together in harmony. She was my aunt, but I didn't know her well until I got married. She lived in Aleppo while I was born and raised in Istanbul. We could have had problems when living together, but it didn't happen. We always loved and respected each other. She was more like a good aunt to me than a mother-in-law. She was like a foster mother during my years in a foreign land.

So, she wasn't born in Aleppo but went to live there later?

Güzîde Çelebi: No, dear. My maternal grandfather Mehmet Bey is a Cherkes prince, of an origin called Abkhazian Merçen. He was abducted and taken to Istanbul. His paternal aunt was then working at the palace in Istanbul, she used to keep the keys to the place where the jewels are kept. When she heard the news, she sent all the men at her service and had her nephew located. She took my grandfather to live with her, not to send him back again, enrolling him to a military school in Istanbul. Back then he didn't even speak Turkish, but in time he grew to be a good soldier. When he was a major -apparently it was a quite valued title at the time- he was sent to Aleppo as a "Commandant of Extraordinary" (Military governor of Aleppo). It was Ottoman times, everyone was there in Aleppo for a duty, and they knew each other well. In these years, my grandfather Cherkes Mehmet Bey was very good friends with my grand-grandfather Ali Muhsin Pasha, later marrying his daughter to have nine children. Most of these children became martyrs to their land. Their graves are in these lands. Like my mother, my mother-in-law (İzzet Hanım) was also born in Aleppo. All the siblings got married to Turkish people. They didn't mingle a lot with Arabs but knew them well.

Can you share with us some memories of Esin Çelebi in Aleppo?

Güzîde Çelebi: There was a small age difference between our mother and her aunt, so we used to call her "little mother".

She had married in Antakya. Her husband was among the notables of Antakya and used to live there. She had one daughter and two sons. The sons were much older than us. One of them was a member of parliament. Each child spoke two-three languages well, they played piano, and rigorously performed their worship and rituals like ablutions.

The daughter, sister Tiraje, was so careful in a way not to use money brought by peasants before washing and drying it. And there was this girl Zeynep, who was raised by sister Tiraje. They asked her to watch after Esin. As the family was living in a big house, they warned Zeynep to accompany Esin all the time. During one of our visits to them, I guess Esin was three back then, we had ice cream in the evening. Esin vomited the moment she had the ice cream. All the family was panicked, wondering what happened to her. There are a lot of doctors in the family. They arrived to check Esin to see why she vomited. Some said: "Well, the ice cream was cold", although she hadn't eaten much of it. Finally, Zeynep said: "My sister had washed money, and we had put them on a paper to let dry. I saw Esin playing with the punched coins." They immediately checked and counted the coins and saw that one of them was missing. The coin was located in Esin's throat when they took her to X-ray. One of these old punched dimes was sitting there. A doctor advised to take her to Aleppo immediately, saying: "There is an Armenian doctor in the hospital there, our family doctor Altunyan. He is the only one who can safely take the coin out, don't let anyone else try that." We called her father to give him the news and let him know we were coming. At the time the Turkish-Syrian border was closed from both sides in the night.

Was the border closed in the evening?

Güzîde Çelebi: The border was closed at midnight, after 12:00 AM. And it was already evening before we settled things. We got in the car, Esin fell asleep on our way. Meanwhile, her late father had found the doctor and told him what happened. So, he waited at the hospital in the evening to examine this interesting case. As soon as we arrived, the doctor located the coin and said: "Here it is, it got stuck in here. Nothing will happen until the morning. She can sleep. I will take it out early in the morning." So, we went back home. Esin slept, but we didn't. We stood by her to see if she could safely breathe. The doctor arrived in the morning and took Esin to hospital. He didn't want us to come in. He took the coin out of her throat. Consider that it turned all green before it had been 48 hours, think how much our stomach can work to save us from strange objects. That coin hadn't even reached the stomach. The doctor used a different type of medical instrument to take it out from the mouth. At the time it was a newly developed instrument which was not normally available in Aleppo. But the doctor's son had happened to bring it from the United States during one of his travels. We were all happy in the end. Esin was totally fine immediately after, she was playing like nothing happened.

So, there was this swallowed-coin incident. But Esin was a good, well-behaved child. She didn't upset us. She used to speak half-Arabic, half-Turkish when she was a child. Antakya has a famous spot (Harbiye). I think it is the beginning of the Asi River, where the flow almost takes the form of a waterfall. Once she joined a visit there, and in the evening, she was excited, describing the scene like:

"Mother, *ma*[1] was flowing in the place I've seen today!" As a child, she used to have such hybrid sentences to express many other things.

Photograph 8: Esin Çelebi, her mother Güzîde Çelebi and father Celâleddin Çelebi (Aleppo 1950).

Esin Çelebi: My mother's friends in Aleppo were all Turkish. There were a lot of Turkish people living there at the time of my childhood. We spoke Turkish at home, and my mother's guests were Turkish. There were also Cherkes people. My paternal grandmother used to join their social gatherings as she was half Cherkes on her father's side. The Cherkes have a branch called Merçen, which was my grandmother's origin. Merçens were considered blue blood. So, my grandmother was respected a lot in her social circle. Whenever we joined a meeting, people around, even including old ladies, stood up to greet and make sure we had a seat. I used to feel flattered and embarrassed at the same time, while grandma and myself were both hosted in the seats of honor.

1 Translator's Note: "ma (ماء)" means water in Arabic.

We had a steward (*vekilharç*) to take care of the house and run errands like shopping: Abdülhamid. He used to wear a red tarboosh (*fez*) and a three-piece suit. And there were Sufi elders (*dede*) in Aleppo when I was a child. While at service, they used to wear traditional Mevlevî ritual hats (*sikke-i sharif*) and garments (a *service* gown called *tennûre* and a dervish jacket called *hırka*). There was no legal ban or restriction on a particular dress code in Aleppo[2]. Among our guests, there were some Arabs, wearing long white robes (*entâri*) and their traditional headdresses (a square scarf called *kefiyyeh* is secured by a black band called *igal*). They used to visit my father, sitting and chatting in his study room. So, we had guests from diverse backgrounds. It was colorful.

Can you talk about the days after you returned from Aleppo? When did you come to Istanbul?

When I reached school age, my family brought me and my brother Faruk Hemdem Çelebi to Istanbul to live with my maternal grandmother. I started to attend Fevziye Schools Foundation Işık Private High School. And Faruk Çelebi, 21 months younger than me, started to attend kindergarten. My grandmother was living with my aunt, so we started to live with them in Istanbul during the winters, and back in Aleppo during the summers.

How long did it last?

For four years. It was a summer afternoon in 1958; my father came home. My grandmother, my mother and he talked.

2 Translator's Note: Certain accessories like Fez and Turban were banned or restricted in Turkey since 1925 Hat Law.

Then we started to pack. With as much as a car can take, we left the house late in the night, and never returned to Syria.

Güzîde Çelebi: Turkey, Iraq, Iran had an agreement at the time. Arabs didn't favor it, so they wreaked havoc. First, there was a revolt in Iraq. Then they killed the king's surrogate, afterwards dragging his body in the streets, and then doing the same to King Faysal. They pillaged the properties of the rich, killing them all. They began to walk in the streets, shouting slogans. All that happened was exactly what I was afraid of.

Esin Çelebi: My father was born and grew up there, so he had a lot of friends around. Later I learned that his friends, people of high rank, had called my father and warned: "Hurry up! Pack your family and leave Syria right away. They are plotting a rebellion against Turks. There's no way we can protect you." So, we left home in half a day.

Here I must share a sad memory. My father had bought me a book, for he knew I loved reading. It was a tome with a red hardcover, not quite portable, but something that I could only read at desk. Its name was One Thousand and One Arabian Nights. Each tale started with a miniature painting. On that day, I left that book on the desk in Aleppo. I have many books now, but I can't forget that one.

You left home in such a hurry...

Yes, indeed... We left Aleppo in a big rush in 1958 and never went back there. I haven't been to Aleppo since then; no contact. I had my aunt there, who arrived in Istanbul shortly after. Her two daughters had moved to Beirut. So, we didn't have anyone staying there.

Güzîde Çelebi: Yes, we moved to Istanbul in 1958. My youngest daughter Gevher wasn't born at the time. We didn't have much difficulty adapting as all the family were already here. In prior years we used to bring our children to visit my mother frequently anyways. And we had already enrolled them in Işık Private High School due to the law requiring all Turkish children to attend Turkish primary schools.

Was the Mevlevî House in Aleppo active at the time of this incident? What are your memories from there?

No, the Mevlevî House was closed prior to that incident. In 1945 Sadullah Cabiri and his cabinet, ruling Syria at the time, decided to officially abolish the *Chalabi* post and then confiscated the assets of the foundation. My father Celâleddin Çelebi was offered to get back all his property under the condition that he become a Syrian citizen, which he rejected, stating "I am a Turkish citizen!" So, his entire property, both possessions and land, were seized. But the Mevlevî elders *(dede)* were allowed to stay in the Mevlevî House for as long as they lived. They were also provided with a minimal salary. The Mevlevî House in Aleppo was closed after they passed away. The complex was then converted to a mosque.

Güzîde Çelebi: I remember once staying in the Mevlevî House when I was a child. It was during one of our trips to Aleppo, where my aunt İzzet Hanım was living, so we were visiting her. When I went back after I got married, it had been a long time since the Mevlevî House was closed.

There were three dervishes, who were called *dede*: Râşit Dede, Ferhat Dede, Gâzi Dede. They came from the Mevlevî

Houses in Turkey after enactment of the Law of Dervish Lodges in Turkey.

Photograph 9: Celâleddin Çelebi with Mevlevî Dervishes (*Dede*).

Ferhat Dede, I guess he came from Afyon... Râşit Dede was initially been Armenian, later to become a Muslim. His good progress under this new tutelage eventually brought him the title *dede*. Nobody challenged him: "You are an Armenian, how come you are like that now?" He used to visit us and cook for us, and he was very good at that. But the real cook was Gâzi Dede. He was the cook of the dervish lodge.

My father, grandfather, uncle and great uncles... Now they rest in *hamushan*, the cemetery of that Mevlevî House. I don't know how to locate the grave of my father. I hope the situation in Syria stabilizes soon, so we can go there and find his grave.

My son Faruk Hemdem Çelebi says: "Mother, don't worry. They took the Mevlevî House as a central reference point. East of the Mevlevî House was demolished, but the west side is intact. So, the dervish lodge remains." I hope so. Dervish rooms, later turned into shops, and all the market and bazaar were on the east side, we used to reach the dervish lodge by walking the path inside there.

Esin Çelebi: When the Mevlevî House was closed, they provided my father with a salary and gave him a flat within one of the buildings of the foundation. I was born and grew up in that flat. Later they asked for rent and also withdrew the salary. That's another story, what the Arabs did! They both confiscated the Mevlevî House and its revenue stream. They didn't allow any newcomers but only permitted certain dervishes (*dede*), who were already living there, to stay there for as long as they lived. My father Celâleddin Bâkır Çelebi used to describe his life there with these words:

"... the Mevlevî House was segregated into *harem* and *selâmlık* sections. Me, my sister, father, grandmother, uncle and two aunts, we used to live in the *harem*. So, this section made our home. *Selamlık* was located in a yard, which was separated from the *harem* with a gate. Private rooms of the dervishes who completed the initial 1001-day training, their classrooms, the library, the kitchen (*matbah*) and the *semâhâne* (the hall where the *semâ* ritual is performed) were in that section. The Mevlevî House was like a school, where the Mevlevî manners and rules of conduct (*usûl and âdab*) were taught, Quran *tafsir*s and Masnavî readings were performed, hadiths were recited, and studies of music were conducted. Also, Turkish culture was largely promoted: most important of all, only Turkish was spoken there. To instill a certain cultural awareness, the gardener dervish used to cite and teach local names, that of trees, cities and districts, whereas the chief cook (*aşçı dede*) used to teach Turkish cuisine, like how to cook some local dishes."

Speaking of the chief cook, I must also tell the story of Celâleddin Çelebi's first encounter with Mevlevî cuisine. When he was a 6-7 months old baby, on a day when his *lala* (male nanny) took him to the yard for a stroll, some elder dervishes saw him and immediately took him to the kitchen (*matbâh-ı sharif*). There they spent a jolly good day, which customarily involved the ritual slaughter of an animal, followed by cooking *halva* (a traditional semolina dessert) and doling out money to the dervishes (another Mevlevî tradition, called *niyaz*). Finally, photographs were taken on the chief cook's post before the baby was handed to his mother, and the day was ended with a *semâ ritual*. Later, this was repeated several times to have an occasion to cheer up. Celâleddin Çelebi later told us that as he grew up a bit, he started to visit the kitchen himself to seek refuge there, giving way to new occasions of fun. As he mentioned these days, he always spoke very highly of the dervishes who took care of him, especially his *lala* Abdülhamid, Gâzi *Dede*, Ferhat *Dede* and Raşit *Dede*.

Photograph 10: Celâleddin Çelebi when he was a baby.

Was the Mevlevî House in Aleppo the central type called Âsitâne?

Yes, it was an Âsitâne. Atatürk and Abdülhalim *Chalabi*, the father of my grandfather, had a conversation before the banishment of the Mevlevî Houses in Turkey with the enactment of the Law of Dervish Lodges. Atatürk invited Abdülhalim Chalabi from Konya to Ankara and said: "We will have to close the Mevlevî Houses as we can't make an exception to the law. But I believe that Hz. Mevlânâ's spirit will encompass the world day by day."

Then, by a mutual decision, Abdülhalim *Chalabi* sent his son, my grandfather Bâkır Çelebi to the Mevlevîhâne in Aleppo as *sheikh* when he was only in his twenties. Abdülhalim *Chalabi* passed away a short while after the closure of the Mevlevî Houses in Turkey. After that, the *sheikhs* of all the Mevlevî Houses outside Turkey started to follow Bâkır Çelebi. This is how the Mevlevî House in Aleppo became a major, central seat of the tradition (called *Âsitâne-i Âliyye*).

Photograph 11: Celâleddin Çelebi with his *lala*, Abdülhamit *Dede*.

ISTANBUL

Can you talk about your life after your return to İstanbul?

Güzîde Çelebi: We moved to a place close to where my mother lived after we came to Turkey. Before our move, we had already brought Esin and Faruk Çelebi to İstanbul to live with my mother Nüzhet Hanım and my sister Meziyet Hanım. They started to attend Işık Private High School. We had our other children enroll in the same school. While I was taking care of the house and the school matters of our children, their father was taking care of the lands in Syria that we inherited from our grandfather (Cherkes Mehmet Bey). Meanwhile, he was carrying out his studies of the Mevlevî order during his time in Istanbul.

So, all five siblings went to the Işık Private High School?

Güzîde Çelebi: Esin and Faruk attended from primary to high school and graduated from there. Emel, Neslipir and Gevher attended and graduated from the primary school there.

All of your family went to the Işık Private High School. Your husband is a graduate. Now your two grandchildren are attending there. We understand that you have been serving in the alumni association for long years.

After eleven years as a student, I spent a long time working in the alumni association. Then my friends asked me If I could lead the effort of building an alumni clubhouse. I worked on that project for about ten years, both for the construction of the building and later for the management of the clubhouse. When everything was up and running in good order, I felt I had completed my mission. Willing to hand over to younger people, I asked permission to leave the board and the association. But my friends insisted, suggesting "At least serve for one more term as president." When I looked into the association's past record, I noticed that although the school was co-ed, there was not a single female president throughout the school's entire, long history. I, therefore, accepted to serve for a term and became the first female president of the alumni association.

Photograph 12: Esin Çelebi Bayru at her study desk.

By the way, the school was originally called Şemsi Efendi School; this was the name at the time Atatürk attended. Having been established by Turks in Thessaloniki, the school was then moved to Istanbul, to be opened in the Laleli district under the name Feyziye School. Later the school was moved again in Istanbul, this time to the Nişantaşı district and its name was changed to Işık Private High School with Atatürk's endorsement.

There's a telegram sent by Atatürk to celebrate the new name of the school. Two years ago, the president of the Feyziye Schools Foundation gave it to me as a new year's present with a note attached. This document is really so precious for me, it is special.

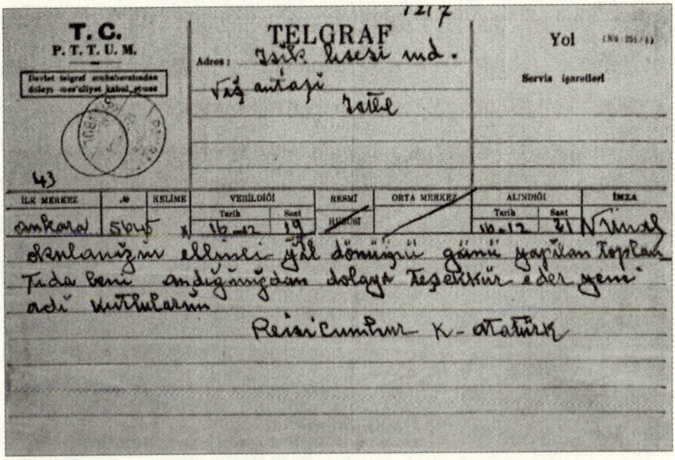
T.C.
P.T.T.U.M.
Devlet telgraf muhaberatından dolayı mes'uliyet kabul edilmez
TELGRAF
Yol
Servis işaretleri
Adres: Işık lisesi md.
Nişantaşı
İstanbul

İLK MERKEZ	No	KELİME	VERİLDİĞİ Tarih	VERİLDİĞİ Saat	RESMİ / HUSUSİ	ORTA MERKEZ	ALINDIĞI Tarih	ALINDIĞI Saat	İMZA
Ankara			16-12	19			16.12	21	

okulunuzun ellinci yıl dönümü günü yapılan toplantıda beni andığınızdan dolayı teşekkür eder yeni adı kutlularım

Reisicumhur K. Atatürk

Photograph 13: Atatürk's telegram.

I am no longer on the association's board, but my heart always remains there at my school. I try to partake in the activities. At the moment, we have a female president again. Together we keep exchanging ideas, like opinions on ways to tackle some challenging issues.

Both my husband and our two daughters attended Işık intermittently. Now one of my grandchildren started to attend in the sixth grade. He is happy to "go to grandma and grandpa's school this year".

I occasionally visit the school to give speeches, where I always prefer to be accompanied by my grandchildren. They sit with me at the same table. I use PowerPoint slides so that they come with me to help me out with that. That way, they listen to the speech, which is both good for me and them.

You studied Arabic and Persian Philology at university. Was there a particular reason for choosing that field?

That was my father's wish. And it turned out to be very beneficial for me. Yet, my university years coincided with a rough, challenging time in terms of politics and security in Turkey. Istanbul University was threatened by acts of anarchy, the school was subject to attacks both by '*leftists*' and '*rightists*', leading to the cancellation of exams and irregular classes. Students even killed each other over ideological clashes. Overall, it was a difficult time. In these years, I got engaged and then married. Although I was pregnant with our first daughter, I was adamant to keep up my efforts toward graduation despite the challenging environment. It was when I only had my final exams left to go, that one of my instructors said: "Even if you don't have any compassion for yourself, at least consider the baby you are expecting. Go home now. This anarchy will come to an end sooner or later. You can come back and finish your education when things settle." That was 1972. In time, my student registration expired, while my mother kept wishing: "Daughter, you must graduate from university." Then, on an early morning three years ago, my mother called me: "Daughter! I've got good news; there's an amnesty." As I was away, she sent my sister to find my registration records. So, upon my mother's wish,

I re-registered, and now I'm a student taking the finishing exams of Istanbul University, Arabic and Persian Philology Department.

We were talking about the pleasant and positive atmosphere at home in your childhood. Obviously, the family taught their children culture, manners and etiquette. There's a spiritual aspect of this discipline, as well as the aspect on rules of conduct (erkân-edep), including the semâ ritual. When did you and your siblings learn the semâ ritual?

I recall the first ceremony I attended. It was about 60 years ago, quite a long time. I was a child then. We were living in Istanbul, and occasionally visiting Konya for ceremonies. My paternal grandmother used to take us there by train. Those journeys were full of joy and excitement. I never lost that spirit, it is still alive today.

Back in 1958, I was nine years old when my father asked me and my brother to learn *semâ*. Our first *semâ dede* was Resûhî Baykara *Dede*, son of the *sheikh* of the Yenikapı Mevlevî House (Nâsır Abdülbâkî *Dede*). It is not an easy task to learn and perform *semâ*. The younger generations today are learning it the easy way. In our time we spent long hours, standing and turning barefoot on wooden blocks, trying not to step on the nails hammered into them. Only after we had mastered that, did our training continue on normal floors, where we also began to wear our ritual robes called *tennûre*. People get horrified at the thought of a 'nailed wooden block', but they shouldn't. It is a necessary tool to learn about balance.

My brother and I worked really hard. One day, they told us that it is time to join the ritual area (*meydân-ı sharif*).

We prepared for a graduation ceremony at Konya. We had our ritual robes and all other clothes tailor-made for us. Everything was ready.

Our grandmother took us to Konya just in the *Shab-i Arus* week in December. Mehmet Önder, who was the Director of the Konya Museum[3] at the time, had the kitchen (*matbâh-ı sharif*) opened and cleaned for us. Together with the elders, the whirlers (*semâzen)* and the musicians *(mutrib)* we visited the kitchen. My brother and I were in our traditional costumes sewn for the occasion. While the group was singing a traditional hymn (*niyâz ilâhîsi*), we performed *semâ*. Then we greeted everyone, kissing their hands. While they were waiting aside in a traditional *niyâz* position, one of the dervishes (*dede*) said, "How lucky we are... Today, two of our *chalabi*s will join us on the *meydân-ı sharif.* We will perform our *semâ* around them."

Another *dede* objected: "No, Esin Çelebi can't be on the *meydân-ı sharif.*"

When asked why, he explained: "It is against our tradition to have women perform *semâ* on the *meydân-ı sharif.* It is unheard of."

Then others suggested: "These two siblings, don't they just look like twins? Let her join."

Faruk Çelebi and I did really look like twins, except that I had two thick long braids versus his very short hair. We still look like each other today, though not quite like twins anymore.

They said: "Well... We can fix her hair, tuck it in a hairnet and once she wears the big *sikke-i sharif* (traditional Mevlevî hat), no one can tell."

---

3 Translator's Note: The central Mevlevî House in Konya was closed upon the Law of Dervish Lodges in 1925 and converted to a museum.

Another one opposed: "What if it falls down and reveals her hair? They would say 'Look! They are having women on the *meydân-ı sharif*!'"

I was silent, just waiting on the side while the elders were discussing us. This is what we learnt as a rule of conduct (*âdap*) growing up. Then I thought, maybe the only problem was my hair? So, in a whispering tone, I uttered: "I am willing to get a haircut." All the faces turned to me, and the verdict was given: "Esin Çelebi can't be on the *meydân-ı sharif.*" Looking back, I recall feeling upset only for a split second. I instantly accepted. *As the elders decided to do so, let it be*. Perhaps one may have thought: *I am the daughter of a Chalabi, I can do as I wish*, but it didn't even cross my mind. I said *Eyvallah,* which means *all right, agreed* to my elders' decision. Looking back, I am very happy that I upheld the tradition.

I never appeared on the *meydân-ı sharif* since then. But this has taught me something beautiful. I understood, I felt in my bones that *semâ* is performed preferably with the soul anyways, it is the soul's dance, it is a spiritual reverence filled with joy and divine love. I noticed that in all *semâ* rituals, my soul was with the *semâzens* on the *meydân-ı sharif,* whirling jubilantly, even if my physical body was not there. The divine love... As long as it is not taken away from me...

My only sorrow is that ten years later, I saw a woman on the *meydân-ı sharif* in a *semâ ritual* performed at the Galata Mevlevî House. She was a disciple of the *dede* who was the primary opponent of me setting foot on the *meydân-ı sharif* as a girl. She had one thick braid, outside her hat (*sikke-i sharif*), flowing down her shoulders. And the *dede* was with her as the leading whirler.

Photograph 14: Faruk Hemdem Çelebi, performing semâ in his childhood years.

So, there are two kinds of rituals: Âyin-i Sharif and Âyin-i Cem.

Âyin-i Sharif is a ritual that narrates self-discipline (*tazkiyah al-nafs*) through symbols. It is not a show, but a form of *dhikr* (prayer, remembrance of Allah). We can think of the Mevlevî Houses as a boarding school for boys, and *Âyin-i Sharif* as a ritual of this school.

Semâ was also taught to women; they were not left out of this. Indeed, disallowing women from the Mevlevî Houses, or from the *meydân-ı sharif* is neither a Mevlevî rule, nor does it have roots in Muslim or Turkish traditions. Instead, gender discrimination was a prevailing culture in the world in that era. When we look back, it's not even been 200 years since girls were sent to school, there were no schools for girls in those times. There is a section for ladies (*mahfili*) in the Mevlevî Houses, in which ladies have always listened to the traditional music and performed *semâ* among themselves. During *Âyin-i Cem* rituals, Mevlevî elders were known to sit with ladies, engage in conversation with them, listened to the *sheikh*'s religious discussions, sang hymns with delight and performed *semâ*.

Güzîde Çelebi: Faruk and Esin Çelebi are both whirlers (*semâzen)*, Resûhî Bey was their *semâ dede*, he was quite a disciplined person, may Allah bless his soul. He used to carry a stick, with which he used to gently touch our children to warn them in case their arms fell to a wrong position. This was how they learnt *semâ*. Esin Çelebi was not on the *meydân-ı sharif* but Faruk Çelebi joined many *semâ* rituals over the years. Time flies.

The German Orientalist Helmut Ritter's article describing a ritual back in 1960 says: "Faruk Hemdem Çelebi, age 9, also whirled. There was also Şemsi Susamış (age 14), he too was in brand new clothes sewn by Hemdem Çelebi's grandmother."

Güzîde Çelebi: Şemsi Susamış later offered many valuable services in the way of Hz. Mevlânâ. That year, all whirlers had new clothes. My mother-in-law, İzzet Hanım, taught me how to sew dervish clothes like the *tennûre (*ritual gown*)*, and *hırka* (dervish cloak). There was also Mustafa Holat's father, a tailor in Konya. In one of our conversations, Mustafa Holat said, "If I hadn't become Mevlevî, I would have got stuck in my father's small shop. I am grateful to Allah that now I have everything thanks to Hz. Mevlânâ."

Can you tell us about the post of Chief Master (Maqam Chalabi)?

The first Mevlevî House was established in Konya by Mevlânâ's son Sultan Veled and grandson Ulu Arif Chalabi in order to pass on Hz. Mevlânâ's teachings to future generations. The disciples trained there were then sent to nearby cities to establish other Mevlevî Houses, either in the form of larger and central "*âsitâne*"s or smaller "*zâviye*"s. Geographical expansion of the Mevlevî Houses traced respectively the path of the Seljuk and the Ottoman Empires.

The Mevlevî Order was always chaired by a *Maqam Chalabi*, who comes from Hz. Mevlânâ's lineage. His son Sultan Veled and grandson Ulu Arif Chalabi put Hz. Mevlânâ's teachings into a systematic framework and established the first Mevlevî House in a complex adjoining Hz. Mevlânâ's tomb. Then other establishments followed. Chief Masters have always been elected among the direct descendants of Mevlânâ. Also, special care was always taken that the elected person is fit for the post, having sufficient knowledge as well as good management skills. It started like that and has become a tradition since then. All the Mevlevî *sheikhs* were appointed from one center. In the Mevlevî Order, a *sheikh* can't authorize others. The authorization to serve as *sheikh* had always been issued centrally, in written form, only by the *Maqam Chalabi*.

Today, the *Maqam Chalabi* post is a spiritual and symbolic position. After the closure of the Mevlevî Houses in Turkey, the one in Aleppo, Syria became the center and my grandfather Bâkır Çelebi continued to serve from there. This was in accord with Atatürk's wish too. He wanted the Mevlevî Order to somehow continue. Because the Mevlevî Houses are centers that communicate and promote the Turkish culture, tasawwuf, and Islam very well.

Upon the early demise of my grandfather, my father Celâleddin Bâkır Çelebi assumed the *Maqam Chalabi* post and served for a while with the support of his uncle Şemsülvâhid Çelebi. Later the Syrian government also closed the Mevlevî Houses, seizing all the assets, claiming it to be "a Turkish Order". The Mevlevî Order has a certain place in Turkish culture and tradition. My father worked in cooperation with universities and ministries of culture for communication of the tangible, scholarly aspects of this spiritual discipline. And today, through the activities of our foundation, we work in an effort to pass the knowledge on to future generations.

Abdülbâki Gölpınarlı, states the following in his book "Mevlevî Order after Mevlânâ": Upon the decease of Abdülhalim Çelebi, his son Muhammed Bâkır Çelebi took the post of Chief Master (Maqam Chalabi). His brother Şemsülvahid Çelebi acted on his behalf for a while. After Bâkır Çelebi's death in 1943, Şemsülvahid Çelebi wasn't recognized as Maqam Chalabi. Following that, as the Syrian Government stipulated termination of the Mevlevî Houses and dervish lodges in 1944, the official Maqam Chalabi post and the Mevlevî order became history[4]. What is the reason behind the conflicting information?

4 Gölpınarlı, Abdülbâki, *Mevlânâ'dan Sonra Mevlevîlik*, p. 180-181, İnkılap Kitabevi, İstanbul, 2009.

Thank you so much for this question. First of all, as engraved on his tombstone, Mehmet Bâkır Çelebi passed away in 1944. My father was 18 when my grandfather passed away. At the time, his uncle Vahit Çelebi was in Aleppo, serving in the Turkish Embassy there. The reason why he couldn't take the *Maqam Chalabi* post was that he was serving the Republic of Turkey as an official. He simply couldn't become the leader of an order, activities of which were terminated in the country that he officially represented. Therefore, my father Celâleddin Bâkır Çelebi was appointed as the *Maqam Chalabi* with the consensus of the *sheikhs* of all the Mevlevî Houses outside Turkey.

My father confirms that as such: "Upon closure of the Mevlevî Houses by the Syrian Government, I was given a flat in the foundation's apartment block. We moved there together with my mother and sister. In the first place, it was given to me, not to my uncle. In the second place, I was provided with a salary. This confirms my official recognition as *Maqam Chalabi*." Upon the decease of Mehmed Bâkır Çelebi, the Syrian Government officially recognized Celâleddin Çelebi as the *Maqam Chalabi*, paying him a salary (200 Syrian liras) for about one year and provided him with a flat, for which they later started to ask for rent.

I also have to bring an important piece of first-hand information to your attention. During a conversation at our home, my father Celâleddin Bâkır Çelebi told the following to Abdülbâki Gölpınarlı: "My dear *hodja*, I would like to provide the correct information about the *Maqam Chalabi* issue mentioned in your book pages 181 and 363; I do not doubt that you will take the right course of action. The last *Maqam Chalabi* was my grandfather Abdülhalim Chalabi.

After his decease, my father Mehmet Bâkır Chalabi, *sheikh* of the Aleppo Mevlevî House was elected. My father passed away on April 23 1944, in Istanbul. Once we buried him next to his father in the graveyard of the Yenikapı Mevlevî House, I returned to the Aleppo Mevlevî House. There, I participated in a ceremony, with which *sheikhs* and dervishes there recognized me as the *Maqam Chalabi*. As my education was not yet completed then, my uncle Şemsülvahid Çelebi helped me and acted on my behalf during those years. His duty as an official at the Turkish Consulate in Aleppo was disqualifying him from assuming the *Maqam Chalabi* position. The new Syrian Government, formed after the withdrawal of the French forces, stipulated the termination of Mevlevî Houses in 1945. However, they continued to recognize me as the *Maqam Chalabi*, provided a salary and a place to live, a flat from one of the foundation's apartment blocks. Today we continue to be at service, paying homage to our lineage."

As *Hodja* listened, his white beard began to shiver; tears were running down his face, passing through the trembling beard. He said, "*Chalabi*, if you let me, I would like to correct this mistake in the new edition of my book." Sadly, he couldn't live long enough to publish the amended version.

When the book's new edition was due, my father consulted Abdülbâki Gölpınarlı's son, Yüksel *Ağabey*, asking whether he could help correct this mistake. Yüksel *Ağabey* said he couldn't make amendments to his father's works, even by adding a footnote. My father was upset by his approach. Unfortunately, the book's new editions keep getting published with this misinformation.

In 2007, Assistant Professor Nuri Şimşekler, chair of the Persian Philology Department at Selçuk University at the time received an invitation from Tehran University to organize a symposium on Abdülbâki Gölpınarlı. As the academicians had certain reservations about traveling to Iran back then, Professor Şimşekler told me that only one instructor from his department, Assistant Professor Yusuf Öz, agreed to go. He said "Dear Çelebi, there's no other way. It's only the three of us who will make it." Up until then, I hadn't travelled abroad to give a public speech. Professor Nuri encouraged me with his words: "You have already been telling us about Abdülbâki Hodja, you can tell the same to that crowd. You will be the keynote speaker, that's all." Somehow, I got prepared, and we went there. When I took the stage,together with the ambassador's translator, I said:

"Right now, we are in a symposium on Professor Abdülbâki Gölpınarlı. I would like to thank you all for that. Everyone will be sharing information about his scholarly side, about his works. But, just as Hz. Mevlânâ said in the first eighteen couplets of Mathnawi, "Every one supposed that he was my good friend. No one tried to find my secrets kept within"[5] a lot has been written and spoken about Abdülbâki Gölpınarlı, including a documentary about his life, including this symposium on his work.

In summary, many people befriended him when he was alive and afterwards. But how many of us searched for the secret of him? Certainly, Abdülbâki Gölpınarlı was a multifaceted

5 Translator's Note: English translation taken from: "Kenan Rıfâî, *Listen (Commentary on the Spiritual Couplets of Mevlana Rumi)*, Trans.: Victoria Rowe Holbrook, Fons Vitae Publishing, İstanbul, 2011".

person. Everyone talks about him in the light of what they could see from their viewpoint. So, I would like to talk about Abdülbâki *Hodja* as I knew him, the one who is alive in my memories."

It didn't work when the interpreter translated Hz. Mevlânâ's couplet from Turkish to Persian. So, I quoted it again, this time directly in Persian, and the hall broke into a round of applause.

The symposium lasted for two days. On the afternoon of the second day, we had visitors, who were *gazelhan*s (people who sang lyrics of Hz. Mevlânâ) that normally refused to participate in meetings organized by government institutions due to their political stance. They visited the symposium to meet me, to pay homage to Hz. Mevlânâ, and they sang *gazels*. In the end, we had such a big event that there was not enough space to host the crowd.

Professor Tevfik Sübhani, who led the organization committee thanked all participants in his closing remarks and added: "The most important speech of this symposium was that of Esin Çelebi. When I was a student, I worked with Abdülbâki *Hodja* in Istanbul; now I am translating his works from Turkish to Persian. Soon, we will get the new edition of Abdülbâki *Hodja*'s 'Mevlevî Order after Mevlânâ' published in Persian. I would like to add Esin Çelebi's correcting remark as a footnote to the new edition."

The anecdote about Abdülbâki *Hodja* and my father, which I also shared in that symposium is now in the Persian copy of Mevlevî Order after Mevlânâ', but not in the original Turkish version.

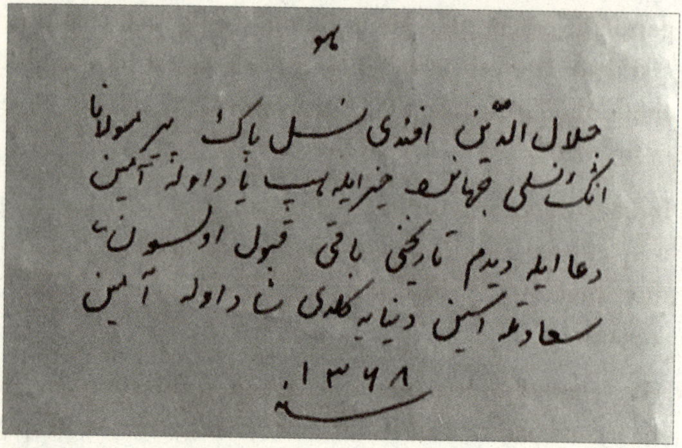
هو
جلال الدين افندى نسل پاك پير مولانا
انك نسلى جهانده هپ خير ايله ياد اوله آمين
دعا ايله ديدم تاريخنى باقى قبول اولسون
سعادتله اسين دنيايه كلدى شاد اوله آمين
١٣٦٨

Photograph 15: Abdülbâki Gölpınarlı's noting down as a record Esin Çelebi Bayru's birth date in verse:

Hu Celaleddin Efendi nesl-i pak-i pir-i Mevlânâ
Anın nesli cihanda hep hayr ile yad ola Amin
Dua ile dedim tarihini Baki kabul olsun
Saadet'le Esin dünyaya geldi şad ola Amin
1368[6]

Translation:

Hu Celâleddin Efendi, Pîr Mevlânâ whose lineage is pristine
May his generations always be remembered in the world with gratitude, Ameen
With prayer I mentioned the date, may it be granted everlasting
In Felicity, Esin is born, may she be blessed, Ameen
1368[7]

As we know, Abdülbâki Gölpınarlı was a friend of your family. When did you meet him?

6 Gölpınarlı, Abdülbâki, *Mevlevîyye ba'de ez Mevlânâ*. Interpreted by: Tevfik H. Sübhani. İntişarat-ı Kayhan, Tehran, 1366 hş.

7 Translator's Note: Esin Çelebi's year of birth, 1949, is 1368 according to the Islamic (Hijri) calendar.

I first met Abdülbâki *Hodja* in 1960, when I was eleven. Looking back on those days, I remember a person who cherished every single moment of his life. I remember his extraordinary look with a boyish, mischievous twinkle in the eye. His shoulder-length blunt-cut white hair had yellow shades from smoking. He had an idiosyncratic style, wearing brightly colored shirts, a black coat in winter, and a wool hat that he tilted to the side.

We know that Abdülbâki Gölpınarlı started attending the Bahariye Mevlevî House at a very young age, accompanying his father. He was so attached to Hz. Mevlânâ that he showed deep respect to us as we were Mevlânâ's descendants. He used to stand up when we entered his room when we were kids. In later years, we watched him treating our children with the same respect.

Abdülbâki *Hodja* was also one of the esteemed scholars who used to visit our house for our Friday meetings. There were occasions we took breaks from these periodical gatherings, usually when my father Celâleddin Bâkır Çelebi was away on a business trip. But Hodja kept visiting nonetheless, probably because he was feeling the warmth of a family with us. His visits were always a source of delight for us kids in the house; we used to gather around him the moment he stepped in.

I believe his inner child never died. I remember the times when he joined us, kids, playing street ball next to our block in springtime. Those encounters with him always delighted us. Because he, the great scholar, always joined our games even if it was for a short while. In his later years, the companionship of his grandson Ali was like a blessing, a true godsend to him.

It was an afternoon in 1964. *Hodja* came to visit us as usual. My grandmother, mother, aunt and us five siblings gathered around him to listen to his stories from The Mathnawi and enjoy some tea. My father was away on a trip. Suddenly *Hodja* gripped his chest and said: "I have a pain, not feeling well." We immediately called the doctor, who was our neighbor. The doctor diagnosed a heart attack and suggested he needed to be taken to the hospital right away, which *Hodja* vehemently refused. In the end, the doctor convinced him to stay with us, so *Hodja* stayed in our house for fifteen days. For me, this turned out to be a blessing. As I was helping my mother while she took care of him, with his food and medicine, he used to call me "My little mother". That was a priceless gift to me. Our mutual respect and love were quite deep and strong. Here I must also mention that he volunteered to be the *hodja* to perform my religious marriage ceremony after the civil one.

Photograph 16: Abdülbâki Gölpınarlı while studying.

Hodja never tried to memorize a single address or telephone number, but rather kept notes in a pocket-size notebook, saying "these things always change". Yet, the great command he had over his chosen subject was amazing. When it comes to that, he used to remember every tiny detail, like "This matter is told in this page of that book in that library, while it is mentioned in this way in this other book, on that page, in that library."

Academicians and researchers of today have it easy. Knowledge is much more accessible in the era of the internet and digitalisation; it is accessed and shared through means like microfilm, photocopies, computers, and also thanks to frequent symposiums. In the old days, *Hodja* worked in freezing libraries, prepared his writings under all kinds of difficult circumstances, edited his work himself, and tried to get his books published in the press houses of the time. So, you can imagine the extraordinary effort it takes to demonstrate his level of productivity (writing so many books) under the circumstances of his time.

Let me also mention; joining him for *iftar*s (fast-breaking dinners) at Ramadan was something I greatly enjoyed. When the official fast-breaking time came (at the sunset), he used to have us wait a little longer- long enough to see the sky turning a dark blue, until the last of the daylight left our sight. Tea and a cigarette were his two essentials at the table. After *iftar,* he used to excuse himself to withdraw in the room we prepared for him for his rest and worship (performing *salat*). He was a good cook too. On a *Ramadan* day, he invited me, my mother and father to an *iftar* at his house. So, we visited him at his wooden house in Üsküdar-Salacak, a district in İstanbul with the best views. A floor table was set in the living room facing the sea; tea was brewing in a teapot placed on a smoking stove. He cooked everything, from soup to dessert, himself. After we ate, he let me clear the table, and it was when I returned to the living room that I heard him saying: "Oh if only I was in my Çelebi's house now..." We were pleased by his subtle way of asking for permission with such a witty remark. My father suggested: "Dear Hodja, please have some rest in your room." Hodja, of quite an advanced age even then, went to his room and half an hour later, he came back, refreshed, and started a conversation. I can't forget the taste of the food he cooked, especially *çilav* - rice cooked in the traditional Persian style.

Later, my father prepared a private room in our house for Abdülbâki *Hodja*, who was in his last years, so that he could work comfortably, especially in the cold winter days. One day, *Hodja* was working in our living room, it was another intensive session where he'd been writing, filling up papers for hours and hours as if in a trance (as I mentioned, he had an amazing capacity to work for long hours under any circumstances). It was then, that my brother Faruk Hemdem Çelebi's three-year-old son Celâleddin ran into the room straight into *Hodja*'s papers, scattering them all around. We were all frozen, mortified. Yet *Hodja* laughed and said, "Oh, dear boy, thanks for reminding me, I worked long enough; it's time for me to rest." Although many who knew him claimed Abdülbâki *Hodja* was quick-tempered, shouting and talking impulsively when bothered, I don't entirely agree. I think there was always a good reason behind his acts of anger. He was especially annoyed by pedantic attitudes of people who were actually quite ignorant. And his temper always faded away as quick as a wink.

He had an impressive depth of knowledge of the Persian language. It was to the extent that it attracted scholars even from Iran to consult him. This is something I heard from his conversations with my father, during which *Hodja* used to tell how these people approached him, including sending letters, and what kind of questions they asked him. There was a Persian scholar that my father hosted in Istanbul, Foruzanfar. On several occasions, my father quoted his firsthand remarks claiming that Abdülbâki Gölpınarlı knows Persian better than himself. When people asked *Hodja* if he'd ever been to Iran, he would comment: "No, it's more like Iran came to me."

Besides his aptitude for scholarship, he was also good at painting and poetry, leaving behind beautiful charcoal drawings, comics and poems. He had the habit of noting down important dates in verse. We know that he left us with an unpublished collection of poems (*Dîvan*), and hope it gets published soon.

What would you like to tell us about your father?

My father Celâleddin Bâkır Çelebi, 21st generation grandson of Hz. Mevlânâ, was born on December 25, 1926, in Aleppo, where the Çelebi family had earlier been sent for spiritual and national duties. His upbringing at home was grounded in Turkish culture and Mevlevî discipline and conduct. Meanwhile, his education at school began in a town school in Syria and later continued in the best French school of the region. He had good command of Turkish, Arabic, and French language and cultures. Apparently and notably, learning Latin helped him to speak multiple languages easily in his later years.

In 1943, Celâleddin Bâkır Çelebi moved to Istanbul, where his father lived. Shortly after, during the 1943-44 term, he started to attend Galatasaray High School. But the same year he moved back to Aleppo upon his father's decease. After graduating from high school, he studied English as well as Law at Beirut American University. Celâleddin Çelebi's spiritual responsibilities increased following his father's demise. He was appointed as the Chief Master (*Maqam Chalabi)* with the consensus of the Sheikhs of Damascus, Lazkiye, Tripoli, Cairo, and Cyprus during a gathering in Aleppo. Due to Celâleddin Çelebi's young age, his uncle Şemsü'l-Vahid *Chalabi* acted on his behalf for a period.

In 1945, the assets of the foundation were seized as the new government in Syria no longer recognized the *Maqam Chalabi* post. The Turkish Government responded to this unfair treatment with nine notes of protest addressing the Syrian Government as well as the French and English forces that were occupying these lands at the time, demanding they adhere to the Treaty of Lausanne, thus returning the assets of Celâleddin Çelebi. These official protests from 1945-46 have remained unanswered to date. However, the Syrian Government officially recognized Celâleddin Çelebi as the *Maqam Chalabi*, assigning him a salary (200 Syrian liras) and provided him with a flat, for which they later started to ask for rent. This was how Çelebi left the Mevlevî House in Aleppo and moved in with his mother and sister.

In 1948, while he was in Istanbul to visit some relatives, Celâleddin Çelebi met his cousin Fatma Güzîde, marrying her soon after. They returned to Aleppo together and lived there until 1958 when they had to leave abruptly upon warnings from their friends to leave Syria right away due to some plots against Turks living there. This is how Çelebi left Aleppo, where he was born and grew up but somehow never felt like home, and came to Istanbul with his family.

Photograph 17: Family photograph

As a result of strenuous efforts, Çelebi sold his lands in Syria to a local person, in exchange acquiring the person's lands in Hatay. Finally, he was back in his homeland. He was engaged in business and agriculture in Hatay, while his children were attending school in Istanbul. During this time, he travelled back and forth across the country, juggling responsibilities of living, settling life in Turkey with new faces and new information as well as living up to a spiritual status in a manner fully compliant with the Turkish law. This was far from easy. But I believe his ancestors gave him a hand tackling this great challenge, for he was on the right path, on such a beautiful path in life.

After he completed his military service, he started to host open house meetings in Istanbul. The house was like an open university, although it was hard to tell who was a student and who was a teacher. Everyone was sharing their knowledge with the utmost decorum. About 60-70 people were regular guests of these gatherings. Among the visitors were many esteemed scholars who were well-pedigreed in Sufi centers (religious and spiritual schools), writers, musicians and people who came to listen, in short, they were all people who loved

Hz. Mevlânâ... Among them, I recall Abdülbâki Gölpınarlı, Refi Cevat Ulunay, Münir Çelebi, Selman Tüzün, Resûhî Baykara, Şerif Abdülmecid, Şerif Muhiddin Targan, Şerif Refik, Ekrem Hakkı Ayverdi, Sâmiha Ayverdi, Şefik Can, Hattat Hâmit Aytaç, Münevver Ayaşlı, Nezihe Araz, Safiye Ayla, Mesut Cemil, Saadettin Heper, Halil Can, Ulvi Erguner, Kâni Karaca, Ahmet Bican Kasapoğlu, Nezih Uzel, Yüksel Gölpınarlı, Üsküplü Hakkı Dede, Bahir Şereftuğ. From time to time Süleyman Hayati Loras, Mehmet Önder and Fevzi Halıcı also travelled from Konya to join these meetings. Whether my father was in Istanbul or not, the house was open to these meetings every Friday. His mother İzzet Hanım, his wife Güzide Hanım and us five children, we were ready to host the guests.

Photograph 18: Esin Çelebi, her grandmother İzzet Hanım, her mother Güzide Hanım and her siblings.

Photograph 19: Celâleddin Çelebi (Esin Çelebi's father) while giving a speech.

My father was always a law-abiding citizen. In order not to make a bad impression and to prevent potential rumors, he made sure he wasn't around in Konya during *Shab-i Arus* (from December 7-17), commemorating Hz. Mevlânâ's death. But once visitors left and the festive hustle and bustle gave way to silence in the city, every year on December 18th, he travelled to Konya to visit Hz. Mevlânâ and shared private moments with his dear ancestor. These were, of course, important lessons for us. While always acting in a lawful manner, he didn't ever back down from his duties. This is how he continued to serve and lived up to his spiritual responsibility after his return to Turkey. He valued literature and science and tried to be of service in that respect.

He worked with the Government, and always respected laws and regulations as I noted. For instance, when he had visitors, even from abroad, he always informed government officials, inviting a listener from among them. Çelebi saw the benefit of his sensibility: In 1978 he received an official invitation from the Government as a speaker to the Commemoration Ceremonies in Honor of Hz. Mevlânâ's Death (Reunion) Anniversary. My father passed away in 1996. We buried him in Üçler Cemetery, Konya. His funeral ceremony was attended by all the Mevlevî dignitaries of the time.

Could you tell us more about the Üçler Cemetery?

There is a grave in that cemetery, the one on the left of the main entrance. There lie three people. There are mixed opinions in different sources; some claim they were men, some others say they were women. It is said that they were three siblings who came from Khorasan to Konya to see Hz. Mevlânâ, while Hz. Pîr walked to God by the time they arrived. The siblings stayed there, where they were buried later when they walked to God. So, this place is called Üçler Cemetery (Cemetery of the Trio). We can make a visit together. My father, grandmother, aunt and some other relatives and family friends are buried there. Talking about the story of Üçler Cemetery, my maternal grandfather who spent most of his life in Istanbul happened to die in Aleppo, to be buried in the graveyard of the Aleppo Mevlevî House, while my paternal grandfather who spent most of his life in Aleppo died in Istanbul, to be buried in the graveyard of the Yenikapı Mevlevî House.

Photograph 20: The Graveyard (*Hâmûşân, or Khamushan*) of the Aleppo Mevlevî House.

My maternal grandfather died of a brain hemorrhage while on a visit to Aleppo, where he had property in the villages. And it turned out to be a one-way trip when my paternal grandfather Mehmet Bâkır Çelebi (former *Maqam Chalabi* at the Aleppo Mevlevî House) travelled to İstanbul for the wedding of his cousin, as on the way to return home his re-entry was refused in the Aleppo border. So he stayed in Istanbul until his death.

Who was appointed as Chief Master (Maqam Chalabi) upon the decease of your father Celâleddin Bâkır Çelebi?

After my father was buried in Üçler Cemetery on April 17, 1996, we gathered in the room of the Konya Museum's Director. The dignitaries said, "It is our tradition. As we bid farewell to our *Chalabi*, who walked to *Haqq*, we have to follow a new one." And they appointed my brother Faruk Hemdem Çelebi, who became our current *Maqam Chalabi*, our spiritual elder.

How does it feel to be a Çelebi, a descendant of Hz. Mevlânâ?

As I was born into this family, Mevlevî discipline and rules of conduct were something I was naturally exposed to, and inherently adopted while growing up. After all, I believe Mevlevî thought and manners are not distinct from the Turk-Islam culture and tradition. Therefore, when we were children, we never had the impression that we were under a special sort of training. Our elders gave us one word of advice: "My dear child, be careful. If you make a misstep, people wouldn't say 'Esin did wrong', they would say 'Look at the behavior of

Hz. Mevlânâ's descendant.' So, be careful and don't make people badmouth your ancestors." They never interfered with our lifestyles, what we have done, where we were going, how we were dressing, what we were eating or drinking... But that single piece of advice was enough to guide our path. While we were already aware of our responsibility, our elders taught us how to handle it the easiest way. Therefore, I am very grateful that we didn't have any trouble in that respect.

Photograph 21: Hz. Ken'an er-Rifâî.

Güzîde Çelebi: We used to have quite large groups of guests on Fridays. Especially the Fridays of the holy month of *Ramadan*, we had our guests gather and eat around two large tables, each with twelve seats, as well as two large *sinis* (floor-table). Our children, while they fasted in *Ramadan*s, used to serve our guests. Beautiful souls visited our house. Among the ladies, there were some disciples of Hz. Ken'ân Rifâî, the ones I immediately recall are Sâmiha Ayverdi, Münevver Ayaşlı, and Nezihe Araz whom we dearly loved like our own sister.

You mean, Sâmiha Anne?

Güzîde Çelebi: O, dear Sâmiha Hanım... All of us greatly esteemed her. Nobody told me to "revere Sâmiha Hanım", but she had such an air that made one feel like the world would come to an end if you wouldn't respect her. She loved me too. So, our fond friendship dates back to these meetings.

I don't recall what was the occasion for our last visit, but there was a discussion about a political party. There I was surprised, as I'd always deemed Sâmiha Hanım to be apolitical. But it was the first, and the last time I'd seen her defending a political party. She must've had a good reason for that. May Allah bless her soul. When our youngest daughter was born, Çelebi had asked Sâmiha Hanım: "Would you name her?" She was pleased to suggest some names, but each carried a little bit too much gravitas for a child. So I kindly said: "Çelebi, these names are weighty, we can't pick any of them." Çelebi considered that and talked to Sâmiha Hanım again. In the end, our daughter was named "Fatma Gevher Çelebi". But when she was a little child, she used to say: "My name is Fatma Gevher Hüdâyar Çelebi" when people asked her name. She heard it from her sisters as a name suggested by Sâmiha Hanım, and quite liked it, so she always cited it whenever her name was asked. Thank Allah, each of our five children grew up without any problem. So many parents out there face all kinds of troubles with their children. All five grew up to be good people, serving their family, ancestors, and nation. May Allah be pleased with them.

Is Hazrat Mevlânâ Celâleddîn-i Rûmî (Mawlana Jalaluddin Rumi) from the Prophet Mohammad's lineage? What do we know about the family of Hz. Mevlânâ's grandfather?

I haven't seen a direct mention of Hz. Mevlânâ belonging to the Prophet's lineage in the resources. However, I've seen references about his father, Bahaeddin Veled the Sultan of Scholars, being a 10th generation descendant of Hz. Abu Bakr from the paternal side.

According to Manaqib al-Ârifin by Eflâkî, Bahaeddin Veled's mother was a princess; she was the daughter of Alaaddin Muhammed Khwarizmshah.

According to Manaqib, she was a very beautiful lady. When she reached the marrying age, the king gathered wise men of the time to consult their opinion as to what type of person his daughter should marry. They said: "This beauty calls for wisdom and knowledge." So they married her to a young scholar of the time. They had a son, born shortly after the scholar walked to Allah. Later, the mother princess held the hand of his 4-5-year-old son, took him to his father's library and said: "Look my son, they married me to your father within these books, these beauties around." And she raised her son in such a way that in the years to follow, he was to be called Bahaeddin Veled the Sultan of Scholars.

It must be amazing to know about a family history spanning twenty-two generations. On the other hand, it must also be bringing serious responsibilities?

There are only a few families in the world who know this much about their origins, and I belong to one of them. Since our childhood we were told: "You carry this kind of blood, so you must live up to it and be of service"- and we were taught how to do that. I am very glad indeed, for I take it as a spiritual gift. I believe, being worthy of this blessing calls for responsibilities, it indebts us with the duty to serve others.

When did you start to gain awareness of belonging to such a family?

Since we were born, we knew we were Hz. Mevlânâ's great-grandchildren. There was the constant mention of Mevlânâ in our house, just like there are discussions of medicine in a doctor's house and law in a jurist's house. We inherently gained that mindset and never saw this as a burden, instead embraced it as a gift. As the Turkish culture largely overlaps with Mevlevî values and tradition, our upbringing was no different from other Turkish children. Only that, when we reached a certain age, my father advised: "Be careful of your behavior and conduct. Whatever happens, keep in mind that others' mistakes are theirs alone, while any wrongdoing of yours would be attributed to Hz. Mevlânâ." We grew up with this ethos but carrying this responsibility never struck us as a burden. We were left free to make our own decision and act, self-guided by the courtesy that our upbringing cultivated in us. There was no pressure or restriction.

Abdülhalim *Chalabi*, the last official Chief Master (*Maqam Chalabi)* within the borders of Turkey, supported Atatürk during the Turkish War of Independence. Awarded with a Medal of Independence with a green ribbon, he was nominated as deputy speaker of parliament on April 24, 1920, in the 1st term of the Turkish Parliament. My family takes pride in this.

Photograph 22: Abdülhalim Çelebi with Atatürk. Photograph and certificate of the Medal of Independence (awarded to people who made important contributions during the Turkish Independence War)

Mevlevî Houses did their part during the National Struggle. On October 8, 1919, *Postnishin Abdülhalim Chalabi* was appointed as a member of the representative committee formed within the Association for Defense of National Rights. Abdülhalim *Chalabi*'s participation in the association had a nationwide impact. A group including the governor of the time, notables and the civil servants of the region gathered in Karahafızlar Madrasa of Konya. During their meeting chaired by Abdülhalim *Chalabi*, the group elected ten representatives to visit Ankara. The representatives (except Abdülhalim *Chalabi* who was a member of parliament) travelled to Ankara on April 19, 1920. Chalabi didn't insist on making his visit depending on receiving an invitation. Nevertheless, they received a telegram from Mustafa Kemal and were allocated a private train. During the second session of the parliamentary meeting, Mustafa Kemal was nominated as the President and Abdülhalim *Chalabi* as the Deputy Speaker.

Besides Abdülhalim Chalabi, his wife Kevser Hanım also supported the National Struggle during the days leading to the Turkish War of Independence, is that correct?

Photograph 23: Kevser Hanım and her grandchildren Revman, Celâleddin, Fatma.

Kevser Hanım, in Konya, was among the ones in the forefront of the Women's Association for Defense of National Rights and the Association for Defense of the Nation. The occupation of Istanbul had been a matter of deep regret for Konya, just like for many other parts of the country. Public demonstrations were held to protest the occupant forces. Kevser Hanım chaired the women's gathering in Konya on January 8, 1920 (January 16th in the records), where it was decided to protest the occupation.

Ladies who were members of the group that organized the protests, namely the Konya Central Committee of the Anatolian Association for Defense of the Nation, penned and published a declaration on behalf of 5,000 women for the freedom and liberation of the country. The declaration was distributed to the British, Italian and French representatives in the city, to the governor's office, and to the 12th Corps Commander Fahrettin Altay. Below the declaration, Kevser Hanım's signature was at the top of the list. She signed it as "On Behalf of Five Thousand Ladies, Chairwoman of the committee of representatives, Kevser *the Master Chalabi's Harem.*"

Later, on March 22, 1920, five thousand women, children and youngsters gathered on the Hill of Alaaddin to protest the occupation and the Entente, where they'd read the declaration sent to commanders of the Allied Nations and to the Governor's office.

The declaration said:

"With request of your refraining from any decision that would dishonor a nation who lived with freedom and independence for more than six and a half centuries -especially when the ancient rights of many small nations are being restored- and given that we deem the rights of the non-Muslims among us as venerable and worthy of respect as ours, there is no way we can accept any terms that would dishonor our nation, terms proposed under the pretense of protecting minority rights. And there is no way we can accept a peace-pact that falls short of warranting strict application of the Wilson Principles and the survival of Turkey as a free and independent nation, with Istanbul as its capital, and within the same borders as before the aforementioned war with the Muslim Turks."[8]

8 Yılmaz, Meşkure, *Konya'da Müdafaa-i Hukuk Cemiyeti ve Mümtaz Bahri Koru*, p. 37-38, Çizgi Kitabevi, İstanbul, 1961.

Abdülhalim *Chalabi* and his family were friends of Mustafa Kemal *Pasha*. They sent a telegram to celebrate *Pasha*'s marriage with Latife *Hanım*. And they used to dine and chat altogether with their wives in *Chalabi*'s chamber when *Pasha* visited Konya with Latife *Hanım*.

I would like to tell an anecdote here. I'd heard this from Atatürk's confidante Kılıç Ali *Pasha*, and I've been coming across it in social media lately as well. Once, when Atatürk and Kılıç Ali *Pasha* were traveling to Ulus via Samanpazarı, they passed by a shop, on the shutters of which an exquisite carpet was hung. Atatürk stopped the car right away as he noticed the carpet, and they went inside. It was a bookshop - one of the few shops that existed in Samanpazarı in these times - that belonged to a bookseller named Ali *Efendi*. When he saw Ata, the bookseller asked with excitement: "What would you order, my *pasha*?", and *Pasha* said they liked the carpet very much. The bookseller explained: "My *pasha*, this belongs to one of my clients. He left it with me for sale as he needed money. I'm not the owner." Noting that a carpet this beautiful was a quite valuable one, Atatürk asked from where the owner might have purchased that. The bookseller cringed with embarrassment: "My *pasha*, the person who entrusted it specifically requested his identity to be kept confidential. If you don't mind, let me not tell you his name." As this intrigued Atatürk, he pressed further: "Boy, perhaps we will want to purchase the carpet. We would like to know who owns it and how much it costs." The bookseller could only say: "My pasha, they are asking for 40 liras", skipping the mention of its owner. But Atatürk went on to insist, until the bookseller had to disclose, hat in hand: "It belongs to Abdülhalim *Chalabi*, my *pasha*." Atatürk was quite touched by that, ordering Kılıç Ali to pay 40 liras to the shop. While Kılıç Ali paid and the bookseller packed the carpet, Atatürk praised Abdülhalim *Chalabi*'s personality: "Though Abdülhalim *Efendi* is in financial straits enough to sell his carpet, yet he still keeps his doors open to everyone." Then he turned to the bookseller: "Look, we are buying this carpet but send it to Abdülhalim *Efendi*'s house, we can pick it up from there. Also, tell him that we will be visiting him for coffee in the evening." Then they got in the car and drove away.

That evening, Abdülhalim *Efendi* personally greeted his guests at the door. As soon as they went inside, they noticed the carpet was behind the door, packed. Abdülhalim *Efendi* suggested: "My *pasha*, you bought the carpet, but it was brought to my house. Let us have it taken to your car." Atatürk replied: "Abdülhalim *Efendi*, the carpet is still ours. But we would like to have our coffee on it in the occasions we visit you." And like that, he had it unwrapped and rolled out back in its place. After they had coffee and a chat, Abdülhalim *Efendi* walked his guests to the door. His attempt "My *pasha*, the carpet...", was interrupted by Atatürk: "Abdülhalim *Efendi*, we are consigning it to you. We would like to find it here and sit on it whenever we visit you." Then they said goodbye and left. And like that, Atatürk managed to find a graceful, subtle way of helping Abdülhalim *Chalabi Efendi*, without taking the carpet from him, trying not to reveal it even to the bookseller.

Eventually, Abdülhalim *Chalabi* gifted that carpet to the Mevlânâ Dervish Lodge in Konya upon his return to the city after completing his mission in Ankara. So he'd chosen to give the carpet back to where he thinks it belongs, avoiding anything that would count as an abuse of a noble gesture, anything that would put him in the position of the carpet's owner. I think this anecdote is exemplary, not only in that it reveals us the humanity of a person that we know as a grand soldier, a great statesman, a reformist leader, but it is also precious in terms of telling us how respectful he was to a *Chalabi*, leader of a religious order, a true devoted soul.

Abdülhalim *Efendi*, a descendant of Mevlânâ... He wore several hats, quite literally. He served as an MP for Konya. He also liked walking around with his traditional Mevlevî hat, *Dastar-ı sharif.* His doors were always open to everyone. He was a generous, intelligent, kind person. Quite well-spoken and straightforward.

He demonstrated to us the grace of a religious leader, who would sell his carpet to be able to sustain an open-to-all dining table. The *sheikhs* and all the religious men who supported the National Struggle meant a lot to Mustafa Kemal *Pasha*. And the *Mevlevî postnishin Abdülhalim Chalabi* was among the top of the list.

He had become the first MP for Konya. This duty in Ankara necessitated a place to reside there. That's how *Chalabi* found himself in financial difficulty and decided to put his carpet on sale, struggling to manage two houses in two cities, one in Ankara the other in Konya.

Atatürk visited the tomb almost every time he'd been to Konya, particularly wishing to be there, saying: "Every time I visit this city, I feel encircled by Hz. Mevlânâ's spirit", asking for a private moment in Hz.'s presence.

August 3-5, 1920: Mustafa Kemal's first visit to Konya.

Bozkır Uprisings are known in history as the first "Konya Incident". *The 1st Bozkır Uprising* started on September 27, 1919, with provocations by a *sheikh*, Zeynelâbidin *Hodja*, fueling public outrage against the National Struggle. This was followed by *the 2nd Bozkır Uprising*, between October 20 – November 4, 1919. In these times, a raider attack aimed to take command of the Governor's office was contemplated by Zeynelâbidin and an organization influenced by him, the Konya Branch of Allied Forces Freedom Party. On May 6, Army Corps and Police Forces thwarted an uprising in Konya by disbanding a crowd of villagers, about a hundred people, who were headed out to the city. Mustafa Kemal travelled to Konya with the aim of making a first-hand analysis of the incident on the premises and providing the public with the needed motivation and support to carry on with the National Struggle. He was welcomed with great enthusiasm on his first-time visit. His public address on August 3, 1920, aimed to raise awareness of the latest incidents resulting from provocations, thereby restoring confidence and support of the people of Konya for the National Struggle. Afterwards, he visited Hz. Mevlânâ's Tomb and met Abdülhalim *Chalabi*, who was then the *Postnishin* and Chief Master of the Mevlânâ Dervish Lodge, at the time he was also the MP for Konya, and the Deputy Speaker of the 1st Parliament.

April 1-4, 1922: Ghazi Mustafa Kemal's second visit to Konya.

During the visit, which took place in April 1922, *Ghazi Mustafa Kemal* and his entourage visited Hz. Mevlânâ's

Tomb and the Dervish Lodge on April 3rd, where they watched the *semâ* ceremony, followed by a lunch at the dervish lodge.

This visit has been told as follows:

On April 3rd, Monday, they were invited to visit Hz. Mevlânâ's Tomb and the Dervish Lodge, which included a luncheon (*Mevlevî lokma*) hosted by the Deputy *Postnishin Sertarîk* Adil *Chalabi*, and the notables of the dervish lodge. Atatürk visited the lodge, although he was accompanied by the Deputy Governor Abdülhalik (Renda), Chief Military Recruiter Rüştü *Pasha* and Range Inspector Kâzım Dirik. *Chalabis* and *dervishes* welcomed their guests in the yard of the lodge, and from there they went straight to the tomb. After the recitation of Surah al-Fatiha in front of Mevlânâ's sepulchre, the group went to the *semâhâne*, where a semâ ritual was performed in honor of the guests. After that, the chief cook Nizamettin Çelebi prayed: "calling upon a glory soon", and the guests were taken to dine (*lokma*) in the chamber of the *Chalabi*. The lunch ended with a coffee service. *Sertarîk* Adil *Chalabi* presented a gift, each guest receiving a copy of the book called *Menâkıb-ı Sipehsâlâr (Sipehsalar's Manaqib)*, translated to Turkish from Persian by Mithat Bahari Beytur. Not yet published at the time, the book was a collection of anecdotes by Mevlânâ. Later, the group visited the ancient monuments and buildings of Konya, including the mosques of Selimiye, Aziziye, Şerededdin and Alâaddin, and *madrasas* of İnceminare and Karatay. During the tour, local historian and County Administrator Hamdizade Abdûlkadir (Erdoğan) presented information about these places.

July 24-27, 1922: Ghazi Mustafa Kemal's third visit to Konya.

This visit took place at the time when the plans and preparations were made for the Great Offensive. On the night of July 23, *Ghazi* Mustafa Kemal completed confidential meetings in Akşehir, the western front, and scheduled an appointment with General Townshend for the morning of July 24 in Konya.

August 19-20, 1922: Ghazi Mustafa Kemal's fourth visit to Konya.

During this visit, the preparations for the Great Offensive was carrying on, and the Akşehir Western Front visit was paid.

March 20-23, 1923: Mustafa Kemal Atatürk's fifth visit to Konya.

Abdülhalim *Chalabi*, together with *dervishes*, welcomed Mustafa Kemal Atatürk at the station. During this visit, Atatürk gave a number of public speeches addressing the ladies, gentlemen, youngsters, and students of Konya. He was accompanied by his wife Latife Hanım, MP for Konya Refik Koraltan, MP for Gaziantep Kılıç Ali, his first aide-de-camp Salih Bozok, Mr. Recep Zühtü the owner of Hakimiyet-i Milliye Newspaper, Mr. İsmail Habib Sevük from Yeni Gün Newspaper, aide-de-camp Muzaffer Kılıç, Commander of the Guard Battalion İsmail Hakkı Tekçe, and his private doctor Mr. Asım. Overall, Atatürk and his companions were greeted with open arms and enthusiasm.

With the invitation of Abdülhalim *Chalabi* Atatürk and his entourage visited Hz. Mevlânâ's tomb, followed by observance of a *semâ* ritual, a concert of tasawwuf music, and finally a meal at the dervish lodge. During this visit, Atatürk also examined traditional ceramics, tiles, and tablets. At the time, evaluation of the abolition of dervish lodges was ongoing. Atatürk's remarks during his next visit reveal to us that back in the time of this fifth visit, he had in mind to re-open Hz. Mevlânâ's tomb as a museum.

January 3-12, 1925: Mustafa Kemal Atatürk's sixth visit to Konya.

Atatürk was again welcomed with enthusiasm. He watched the parade of scouts and students from the balcony of the mansion, which is now Atatürk Museum. Aside from a number of official meetings, he visited his spiritual parents, *Hadji* Hüseyin Ağa and his wife, at their adobe house in the neighborhood of Sedirler. On January 10th, he received and held meetings with a group including the Chief Master (*Maqam Chalabi)* of the Mevlânâ Dervish Lodge, Mufti of Konya, and the city's notables.

October 17-19, 1925: Mustafa Kemal Atatürk's seventh visit to Konya.

He was greeted by the public and the students and visited the Army Inspectorate and Municipality and Turk Centre.

This was the time when the preparations for the Hat Reform were underway. This caused considerable excitement across the whole country. Atatürk was glad to observe that the reaction in Konya was the same.

After paying a visit to Hz. Mevlânâ, Atatürk goes to the *Chalabi Master*'s chamber. The following exchange took place between the two when Atatürk noticed the master's traditional hat (*dastar-ı sharif*):

Ghazi asks: "*Chalabi Master*, would you accept a gift from me?" Abdülhalim *Chalabi* replies with Mevlevi courtesy and humbleness:

"My dear *Ghazi*, I would be honored to be crowned by your gift."

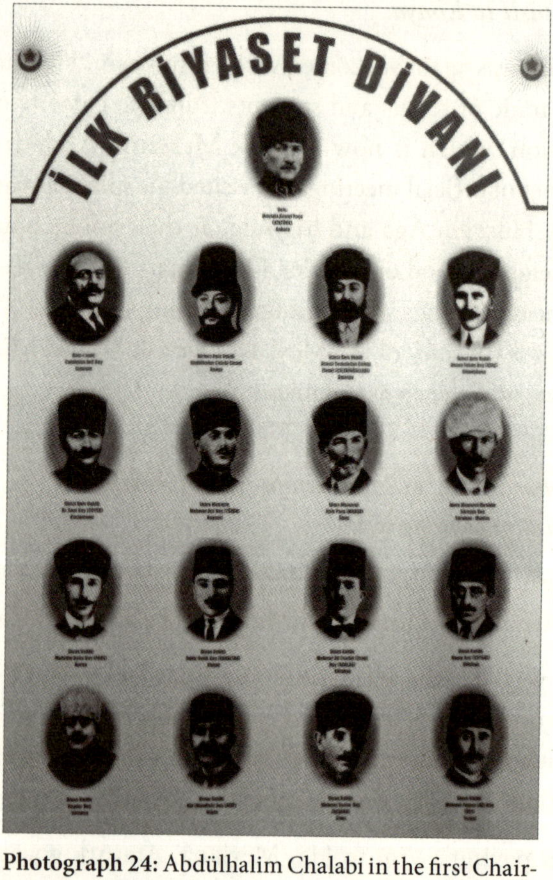

Photograph 24: Abdülhalim Chalabi in the first Chairmanship Council.

So Ghazi orders his first aide-de-camp Major Rüsuhi Bey: "Unwrap the pack and present the gift to Hz. Chalabi." There appears a contemporary hat. Chalabi's master stands up. He takes off his traditional hat. After kissing it and placing it in its storage, he wears the gifted one.

Abdülhalim Chalabi walked to *Haqq* on November 12, 1925. And the Hat Law was enacted on December 13, 1925.

May 18-19, 1926: Mustafa Kemal Atatürk's eighth visit to Konya.

He was welcomed at the station with a big reception, followed by a set of meetings on potential projects for the city. He asked for a number of pure-bred stallions and mares to be sent over to Ankara, so that thoroughbreds in Konya can be raised in the Atatürk Forest Farm. That also marks the year when the Atatürk Statue in Konya was erected.

February 18-Mar 1, 1931: Mustafa Kemal Atatürk's ninth visit to Konya.

He visited the Mevlânâ Museum. After inspecting the works and the plates there, he asked for translation of the inscription above the *niyâz window*, either by Mr. Hasan Âli Yücel (later to become the Minister of Education) or Mr Fuat Gökbudak (the MP for Ereğli), who accompanied Atatürk during that visit.

On that note, Atatürk said: "Well, all the gates are closed but this one. Indeed, during my visit in 1923, I thought we must reopen this dervish lodge as a museum, we must open it to the public instead of closing down. And a year

Photograph 25: The traditional hat (*sikke*) with an inscription of a Persian quatrain.

Derha heme besteend illa der-i tu
Ta reh nebered garib illa ber-i tu
Ey der Kerem-u-izzet-u nur-efşani
Horşid-u mah-u sitaregan çaker-i tu

Translation:

O you (Allah)! The sun, the moon, and the stars are mere servants to your glory, grace, and radiance. All the gateways are closed but yours, so the poor lovers don't lose their way to you.

later (exactly when the Law of Dervish Lodges is enacted), I asked İsmet *Pasha* to convert the Mevlevî Dervish Lodge to a museum, preserving the articles inside. It looks like I carried out the order of this poem. This place has made such a beautiful museum."

Then he wrote and signed the following note on an ornate page in the visitors' book handed him by the museum director:

"I am highly pleased by the orderliness here, which is apparently a work of knowledge." (21.02.1931)

On the same day, during subsequent visits in Konya, he observed the worn-out and neglected condition of the artifacts he saw, leading him to send a telegram to Ankara the next day, addressing İsmet *Pasha*, asking for specialists to be sent to Europe to be trained in repair of the historical artifacts from the Seljuk times. Also, he asked for the establishment of the Association for the Study of Turkish History (later to be renamed the Turkish History Foundation), and a visit by Mrs. Afet İnan and Mr. Tevfik Bıyıklıoğlu for their direct, on-site inspection of the artifacts.

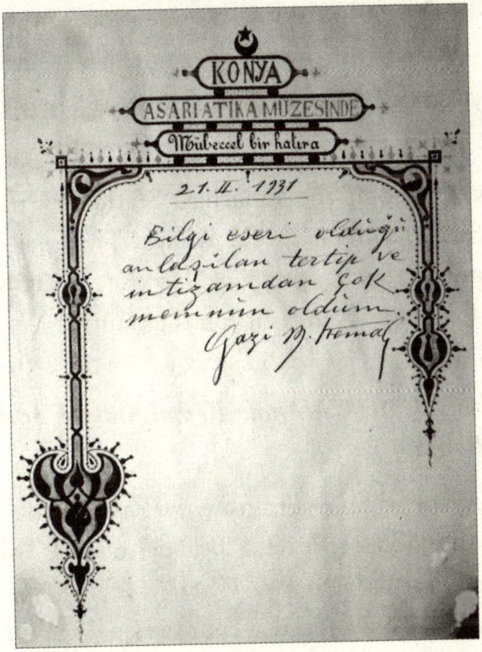
KONYA
ASARI ATIKA MÜZESİNDE
Mübeccel bir hatıra
21. II. 1931
Bilgi eseri olduğu
anlaşılan tertip ve
intizamdan çok
memnun oldum.
Gazi M. Kemal

Photograph 26: The above-mentioned page in the visitors' book.

January 25, 1933: Mustafa Kemal Atatürk's tenth visit to Konya.

He stopped by for a one-hour visit on his way to Adana via train and briefly met people who came to greet him.

February 6, 1934: Mustafa Kemal Atatürk's eleventh visit to Konya.

In his address to the waiting crowd, he said: "The youth of Konya again, like they always did, cheered myself sincerely on. I always have full confidence in the young. The Republic is rising and progressing on your shoulders. From now on, the catalysts for the Republic will not be us; it will be you. Your existence will keep it alive."

January 7, 1937: Mustafa Kemal Atatürk's twelfth visit to Konya.

He was greeted at the Pınarbaşı Station by the Konya Committee and the MP's for Konya. The Issue of Hatay constituted the main agenda of this visit, during which he worked for about seven hours on the train.

November 20, 1937: Mustafa Kemal Atatürk's thirteenth visit to Konya.

He stopped by on his return from the Eastern Anatolia visit. When he was about to leave, a local person said: "My *Pasha*, we would like to listen to you." Ghazi Mustafa Kemal Atatürk responded: "I know you do. Your eyes tell me even if you don't say it aloud. You can rest assured that Hatay will be ours, sooner or later, it will be part of our land."

We do not observe many offshoots in the Mevlevî Order, had the family played any role in that?

There are no offshoots in the Mevlevî Order. The reason is the post of Chief Master (*Maqam Chalabi*). In the Mevlevi Order, appointment and authorization of *sheikhs* can only be made by the *Maqam Chalabi*, *Dastar-ı sharif* can only be wrapped (around the *sikke*, the traditional Mevlevî hat) in case of formal, written permission. *Sheikhs* can not issue authorizations. It has always been the case. However, *sheikhs* can educate proper, eligible candidates as dervishes, they can recommend people to the *Maqam Chalabi*. In some cases, the *Maqam Chalabi* may ask the person to visit Konya to get to know him, to fill in the gaps if any. Only then a *dastar* authorization could be issued.

How is the postnishin appointment made today? The book "Those Who Reach from Mevlânâ to Mawla" cites the names of your friends who serve as part of the Order in Europe.

Mevlevî houses are no longer active, so things are a bit different today. Yes, there are *Sheikh Masters* whom were authorized by my father Celâleddin Bâkır Çelebi and Faruk Hemdem Çelebi. It is important for these people to be well-versed on the religion and the Mevlevî Order. Also their respect and devotion to Hz. Mevlânâ is key.

The authorized *Sheikh Masters* in Turkey are Hüseyin Top, Kadri Yetiş, Nail Kesova, Ömer Tuğrul İnançer, Şemsi Yılmaz Susamış, Emin Işık, Nadir Karnıbüyükler, Fahri Özçakıl, Bahauddin Taha Hidayetoğlu (Çelebi), Hüseyin Erek, Ahmet Sami Küçük, Mim Kemal Öke, Mustafa Holat, Nasır Abdülbâki Baykara, Yılmaz Kafadar, Nezih Çetin.

The authorized *Sheikh Masters* abroad are Kabir Helminski and İbrahim Gamard in the United States, Süleyman Wolf Bahn in Germany, Hüseyin Peter Cunz in Switzerland, Mürsel Marcel Derkse and Yıldırım Ekin in Holland, Mohammad Bordbar in Iran, Mustafa Gustavo Martinez in Colombia, Abdulaziz *Efendi* in Australia. Many of these people came from different religions, later to meet Hz. *Pîr* and learn Islam, to become Muslim, and fulfill the requirements of Mevlevî discipline before starting to raise new students in their countries. These people have been of great service to Islam and the Mevlevî Order. They established associations and foundations under the legislations of their countries. And we, as the foundation, provide guidance, know-how and moral support.

I am currently trying to collect documents for a new book on my brother Faruk Hemdem Çelebi, my father Celâleddin Bâkır Çelebi, my grandfather Mehmed Bâkır Çelebi, his father Abdülhalim Çelebi, and his father Abdülvahid Çelebi. This book will hopefully shed light on the history of the Mevlevî Order during the last century.

Abdülhalim Chalabi's decease caused some speculations, can you provide us any other information? According to the Encyclopedia of Islam, Abdülhalim Chalabi, who honored his family tradition of seven hundred years and devoted his life to serving his country and his nation, fell from the balcony of a hotel room that he occupied in Istanbul. As a result, he went into a coma and passed away at the Yenikapı Mevlevî House, where he was taken shortly after the incident. It was claimed that dizziness caused by diabetes led to the fall, or he was assassinated for political reasons.

In fact, he did not suffer from diabetes; we do not have a diabetes case in the family. But I would like to share an anecdote that I heard from Abdülhalim *Chalabi*'s sister-in-law, Münîre *Hanım*. She was the maternal grandmother of my husband; we lived together for many years. One day Abdülhalim *Chalabi* came from Konya to Istanbul, carrying a medium-sized bag. Handing the bag to his sister-in-law, he said: "Please keep it for a while, I will come back and pick it up." A few days later, he came back to Münîre Hanım's house, had his tea, took back the locked bag, opened it, and showed her what's inside. The bag was full of jewelry and gold, most of which belonged to his family.

Aghast at the sight of the bag's contents, Münîre Hanım asked: "How could you leave this with us?" Chalabi explained: "I entrusted it with Allah in the safety of your house. If you had known what's inside, you would have spent sleepless nights guarding it. I didn't want to disturb you." Then he left with the bag and fell from the balcony the next day. The bag is still unaccounted for. The door of his room was locked, but there were other rooms that shared the balcony from which he fell. Oddly enough, he was taken to the Yenikapı Mevlevî House by unknown persons, who knocked on the lodge's door. Dervishes who were staying in the no-longer-active dervish lodge to perform their last duties overheard the voices and went outside to see the *Chalabi Master* covered in blood, dying. And as soon as he was taken to the *matbâh-ı sharif* (kitchen), the nearest place inside, he passed away. The word was that his hotel, next to Pera Palas, in the backstreet of Beyoğlu, was a place for important people.

Why was he not taken to a hospital? Who carried him to Yenikapı from Beyoğlu, and how, under the circumstances of these days? We were left with so many unanswered questions. At the time, there was no relevant authority to resort to. It was a difficult time for the country too. So it remained a mystery. May Allah bless him with heaven. Whoever did this, they live with this, and God certainly knows about them.

There is nothing else to say.

Bâkır Çelebi, the elder son of Abdülhalim *Chalabi*, was then heading the Aleppo Mevlevî House. Şemsü'l-Vahid Çelebi, the younger son, was in college in France. His two daughters were in Konya, staying with their mother. After the incident, all of them went to Aleppo, to Bâkır Çelebi. It was known that Mehmed Bâkır Çelebi undertook national duties assigned directly to him by Atatürk, and performed valuable work in Aleppo. He had been of great service in the annexation of Hatay to the motherland. Before enactment of the Law of Dervish Lodges, with approval of *Ghazi* Mustafa Kemal *Pasha,* Abdülhalim *Chalabi* appointed his son Mehmet Bâkır Çelebi as *sheikh* of the largest Mevlevî House (*Âsitâne*) in Aleppo. Upon the decease of Abdülhalim *Chalabi* and closure of the Mevlevî Houses in Turkey, the Aleppo Mevlevî House was recognized as the new center. With the endorsement of Mustafa Kemal Pasha, Mehmet Bâkır Çelebi not only carried out his spiritual mission in a region outside the borders drawn by the National Pact (*Misak-ı Millî*) but also, as the public records show, he undertook national duties given the sensitive circumstances of the time, such as his contributions to Hatay's peaceful annexation to our motherland, which was a border dispute with Syria.

In 1939, while he was away in Istanbul, the Syrian authorities prohibited Mehmet Bâkır Çelebi's return to the country, declaring him persona non grata. Mehmet Bâkır Çelebi, who went on to live in Konya and then Istanbul, was assigned a salary (twice the amount paid to MPs) from the discretionary funds by The State of the Republic of Turkey. I think the magnitude of the salary, which was awarded on the grounds of his accomplishments, is proof of the importance of the national duties undertaken by Mehmet Bâkır Çelebi.

On April 23, 1944, he died of a heart attack and was buried in the Yenikapı Mevlevî House, next to his father Abdülhalim *Chalabi*.

Upon the decease of Mehmet Bâkır Çelebi, the *Maqam Chalabi* succeeding his father Abdülhalim *Chalabi*, his son Celâleddin Bâkır Çelebi (1926-1996), who is my father, was appointed as the new *Maqam Chalabi* with the consensus of the *sheikhs* of Damascus, Lazkiye, Tripoli, Cairo, and Cyprus and all the other Mevlevî Houses.

What did you hear from your grandfather about Atatürk?

My grandfather passed away when my father was 17. So, unfortunately, we did not have the opportunity to hear from him directly about Atatürk; what I know is common knowledge.

As known, Atatürk was born in Thessaloniki. It is also said his uncle (husband of his maternal aunt) was a *sheikh* at the Thessaloniki Mevlevî House, and when he was a child, Atatürk used to visit the dervish lodge with his mother. It is also said Atatürk visited Hz. Pîr many times, even requiring to be left alone in the tomb, having private moments of prayer, worship, and contemplation.

Photograph 27: The nameplate "Âsâr-ı Atîka Museum" on the Mevlânâ Museum's main entrance.

The time of these visits also coincided with the abolishment of shrines, but this one, known today as Mevlânâ Museum, was almost never closed.

Except, shortly after the passage of the Law of Dervish Lodges, all the Mevlevî Houses were closed, which necessitated the closure of Hz. Pîr's tomb as an overall complex harboring the Konya Mevlevî House. Soon after that, Atatürk came to visit the place together with a group of MPs and then he ordered its re-opening as a museum. This is how the place was named "Konya Âsâr-ı Atîka Museum." The original name-plate is kept on the main entrance door.

Mevlevî Houses are very important schools with their own libraries, with a curriculum of several universities added together. The books of the closed-down Mevlevî Houses were transferred to the libraries. Meanwhile, the valuable items were gathered in the museum, which has been alive and functioning since then, and for which some improvements are now hopefully underway. A new building reflecting modern museology will be constructed for the exhibition of many precious historical artifacts.

Can you tell us a memory about Mevlevî dervishes, from the times the shrines were closed?

When the Mevlevî Houses were closed in 1925, Mehmet *Dede* (Mehmet Arısoy 1875-1957) was at the Mevlevî House in Konya. His story is a really nice example. Mehmet *Dede* is from Ankara, where he completed his middle and high school education (at Ankara Military Middle School and High School of Government), and attended university. After graduation, he brought his diploma to his parents (he had no money but could not ask for any from his parents either), and traveled to Konya on foot to visit the shrine, to say he wants to be a disciple.

There he was asked: "Did you get the consent of your parents?"

As he said: "No, I didn't," they commented: "That is the most important of all, come back with your parents' consent."

Without money, and without asking any from others, he traveled back to Ankara on foot again. After stating his intention to be a Mevlevî disciple, and having his parents' permission, he went back to Konya, once more on foot.

Like that, Mehmet *Dede* started his education in the Mevlevî House. As he completed the education, he was given a cell to stay in, and he continued to serve and live in the Mevlevî House.

After the closure of the Mevlevî Houses, he was appointed as the watchman of the place. Dwelling there, hosting the museum's visitors (with the help of his foreign language skills), he began to serve as the keeper of the museum and the tomb.

One day, the director told him: "Mehmet, it's time for you to retire."

"Dear director, how so? Retirement from this home, is that even possible?"

"Well, it's over. You've reached the age, you've done everything needed. So, it's time. Look, we can buy you a nice house in a nearby place, you can come and visit whenever you want."

On that, he said: "Dear director, please give me a few days before you sign my letter." "Alright" said the director, unwilling to hurt Mehmet *Dede's* feelings.

After everyone left, Mehmet *Dede* went to the tomb, asking Hz. Pîr: "Where are you sending me?", complaining a little.

That night before dawn, Hasan Âli Yücel (Minister of Culture at the time) had a dream about Hz. Pîr. Hasan Âli Yücel is a Mevlevî disciple, whose education in the Yenikapı Mevlevî House included training in *semâ* in his childhood years.

As Hz. Pîr said in the dream, "Hasan Âli, take care of my dervish," he woke up with excitement, questions swirling in his head. Which dervish did he mean? The Mevlevî Houses had been closed; there was nobody left. Unable to sleep a wink until the morning, he finally decided to call Konya. Using the limited telecommunication means of the time, he called the director in Konya to inquire:

"What's new in the shrine?"

"Everything is fine, sir."

"Tell me," and as the director talked about this and that, he said, "Okay, fine..."

Then he called the Governor of Konya, asking again,

"What's new in Konya?"

The Governor tells him this and that, nothing coming up.

So he called back the director and inquired:

"Tell me what you have done yesterday, what are you going to do today..."

"Well, Mehmet Dede's retirement is due. I will write his letter today, which I was going to do yesterday, but he asked me to wait, so I'm going to take care of that today."

Hasan Âli responded with excitement: "No, don't do it. Wait."

And he, the minister himself, traveled from Ankara to Konya to meet the Governor and the Museum Director, where the three discussed the issue to find a proper solution. Mehmet Dede lived in a room in the shrine until the end of his life.

He had a charcoal burner, with which he enjoyed making Turkish coffee for his guests. He was a very knowledgeable person who really did important services for the Mevlevî Order. I barely remember my encounter with him as I was only a little child. Nevertheless, he had a conversation with me, asking me to tell him about our life in Aleppo, about the dervishes there.

Can you also tell us about other Mevlevî elders and notables that you know?

Let's not limit this to Mevlevîs; our house was open to everyone. After moving to Turkey, we had a lot of guests, especially on Fridays. Whether my father was in Istanbul or not, we used to have many guests. Among the visitors were many esteemed scholars who were well-pedigreed in Sufi centers (religious and spiritual schools), writers, musicians, such as Abdülbâki Gölpınarlı, Refi Cevat Ulunay, Münir Çelebi, Selman Tüzün, Resûhî Baykara, Şerif Abdülmecid, Şerif Muhiddin Targan, Şerif Refik, Kâinat (Büyükaksoy) *Hanımefendi*, Ekrem Hakkı Ayverdi, Sâmiha Ayverdi, Şefik Can, Hattat Hâmit Aytaç, Münevver Ayaşlı, Nezihe Araz, Safiye Ayla, Mesut Cemil, Saadettin Heper, Halil Can, Ulvi Erguner, Kâni Karaca, Ahmet Bican Kasapoğlu, Nezih Uzel, Yüksel Gölpınarlı, Üsküplü Hakkı Dede, Bahir Şereftuğ, not to mention the people who came to listen to them. In short, they were all people who loved Hz. Mevlânâ... About 60-70 people were regular guests of these gatherings. From time to time Süleyman Hayati Loras, Mehmet Önder and Fevzi Halıcı also traveled from Konya to join these meetings. I feel grateful that we grew up in the service of these people.

You remarked, "Let's not limit this to Mevlevîs." Can you tell us about your family's relations with other Sufi orders?

Of course... On the first days of the religious holidays, Sâmiha (Ayverdi) *Hanımefendi*, Nezihe (Araz) *Hanım*, the elders used to visit my father and my paternal grandmother out of respect for their bloodline. On the third or the fourth day of these holidays, depending on the occasion, we used to pay them a visit with my father. Those visits, knowing all those elders, was a true pleasure. May Allah bless their souls. I can't forget Mami[9]. They were all beautiful people. What I don't understand now is the divisive, polarized approach to the religious orders. That's not how we were raised, we've never seen anything like that. We were raised among our elders, whose paths were all guided with the same compass. The divisiveness we experience today doesn't make any sense. Anyways, it is none of our business.

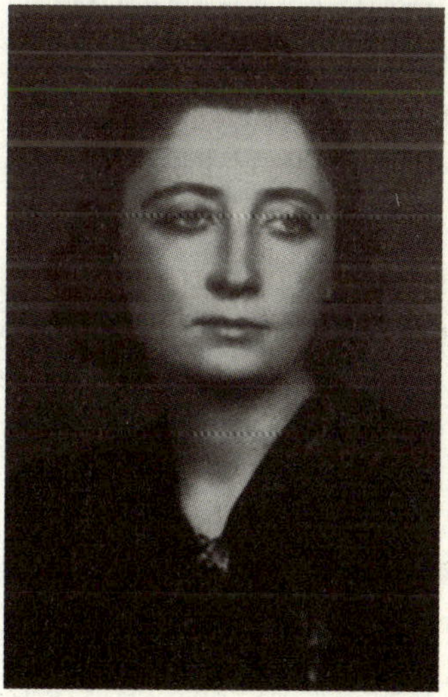

Photograph 28: Sâmiha Ayverdi and Nezihe Araz.

9 Saime Özveren, the fosterling of Nazlı Hanım -an inner circle disciple of Hz. Ken'ân Rifâî-. She was described as "graceful, polite, the epitome of wisdom and divine love" by Sâmiha Ayverdi.

Güzîde Çelebi: We were all very fond of Nezihe Araz. We had wonderful times together. She used to join us when we were traveling to places like Kerpe, to keep us company. We had the best times there, having nice chats. And Sâmiha *Hanım*, for me, was the queen of all the ladies I've known. Ekrem Hakkı Bey and his wife İlhan *Hanım* used to join these visits as well. İlhan *Hanım* reminds me of *sultans*; she was also a very cultured person. All these names were among the guests of our open-house Friday meetings as well.

Esin Çelebi: We knew all of the Ken'an er-Rifâî disciples, and also the disciples of those disciples -almost all of them. We used to visit each other on certain occasions, and joining these get-togethers with my father was a great pleasure.

On which days would these gatherings take place?

There were some private meetings, although I can't quite recall their purpose. I was a child back then. For the gatherings other than the holiday visits, the hosts would greet my paternal grandmother as the guest of honor. And I used to be seated next to her as an homage to my bloodline. May Allah bless them all.

You've just asked: "How was your childhood?" Well, we grew up trying to live up to our bloodline. Our elders reminded us that all the respect that we receive from others is not for the sake of ourselves; it is an homage to our lineage. I am so grateful, may Allah wrong us not. All of our services today are nothing but a blessing of Allah. May the Lord not keep us from serving others. Here I would like to tell you another anecdote if I may. Once, I had an appendectomy, and Sâmiha Hanım visited us afterward. I still keep her get-well-soon present (a beautiful yellow cup) in my display cabinet.

Photograph 29: The yellow cup mentioned as the gift from Sâmiha Ayverdi.

Could you also tell us about your neighbors?

Güzîde Çelebi: Our neighbors were people who cared for each other. Once during the years of Çelebi's military service in a turret deck, our upstairs neighbor Abdülmecid Efendi watches out from the window and sees Çelebi coming home, exhausted. He taps on the window to invite Çelebi upstairs. Covered in dust and dirt, Çelebi first came home to take a shower and let us know he is going upstairs to visit Efendi. As Abdülmecid Efendi asked: "Çelebi, you look so tired. What's the matter?" Çelebi said: "I don't understand. There's chaos in our land." It was before the 1960 coup d'état. At the time, Çelebi was the aide-de-camp of Cemal Gürsel. He was recruited on the grounds of his command of foreign languages. But they were sending him away to Istanbul when there's a need to discuss matters in privacy. Later, we came to understand why. For instance, on the day of the coup (May 27), Çelebi was in Istanbul again. When he was about to return, they commanded him to stay in place. And the coup took place shortly after.

Esin Çelebi: They kept my father away to protect him...

Güzîde Çelebi: *Sharif* Abdülmecid *Efendi* was a descendant of Hz. Muhammad *(s.a.v)*. And his neighbor across the hall, *Sharif* Refik, was another descendant from a different generation. Both were quite dear to us. Abdülmecid *Efendi* used to join our house meetings, while we saw *Sharif* Refik only rarely as he didn't spend a lot of time in Turkey. Both used to speak Turkish like a native. At that time, Turkish culture and tradition had a place in the upbringing of all *Sharifs* and *Sayyids* (honorific titles, referring to the descendants of Hz. Muhammad from the side of his grandsons Hz. Hasan and Hz. Hüseyin, respectively). *Sharif* Abdülmecid *Efendi* was married to Rukiye Sultan *Efendi*, granddaughter of the Ottoman Sultan V. Murat. And his brother *Sharif* Muhittin *Targan* was married to Safiye Ayla, who was a famous singer of Turkish classical music.

Photograph 30: Rukiye Sultan Efendi

Whenever she came to visit her relatives, Safiye Ayla used to stop by and chat with my mother-in-law, before going upstairs. When Abdülmecid *Efendi* passed away, his wife Rukiye *Sultan Efendi* warns Safiye *Hanım*, asking her sister-in-law to change her dress for one that's proper for the funeral home. So, Safiye *Hanım* came downstairs to complain: "What's wrong with my dress? It is an ordinary black one..." It was a black dress, though a floral one with big red flowers. But in the end, she listened to Rukiye Hanım and changed her dress; she was very respectful.

Rukiye *Sultan Efendi* was the daughter of Sultan V. Murat's son. As you may know, in the Ottoman Empire, paternal granddaughters of Ottoman Sultans were called *Sultan Efendi*, while maternal granddaughters were called *Hanım Sultan*. Rukiye *Sultan Efendi,* having spent her childhood there, used to recount the big fire that destroyed the Çırağan Palace. At the time, white eunuchs shouting "*Destur, destur!*", warning others to give way, used to carry lit torches inside the palace. One day a eunuch stumbled on something, causing firebrands to scatter all around. The place caught fire so quickly that they couldn't put out the fire, which destroyed the palace. She used to tell us about that.

Sharif Abdülmecid *Efendi* and Rukiye Sultan *Efendi* didn't have children, but they used to invite our five children to their house from time to time. After tea service, they would give the children a concert: Abdülmecid *Efendi* would play the violin, Rukiye *Sultan Efendi* would join him with her concert piano. They had an old-style car. There were times they invited our children to outings on the Bosphorus. Both were very old. When talking about children, they used to say: "Allah didn't grant us children, but blessed us with grand-children." They had pearly dominoes from Sultan Murat. Sometimes Sultan *Efendi* was playing dominoes with Gevher, who was only five then.

Esin Çelebi: *Sultan Efendi* grew up in the palace. Then she got married and moved to Paris with her husband, who was an ambassador there. Although she didn't face any restriction, she didn't go out much there, remaining a stranger to the world on the outside. When she moved back to Istanbul, she mostly socialized with us. One day, she came downstairs and knocked on our door to ask if she could see my mother. Wondering what she would say to my mother, I greeted her: "Please wait inside, *Sultan Efendi.*" You know, I was a kid. With that curiosity, I found myself eavesdropping. She said: "I apologize beforehand if I'm about to ask anything improper, please forgive me." My mother replied: "Please, please, *Sultan Efendi*, tell me." Still having a hard time talking, she asked: "We were playing dominoes with little Gevher when a piece fell on the floor. While I reached over, she said: 'Never mind Sultan Efendi.' So I wonder what never mind means. Would it be anything obscure?" She was such a stranger to the world on the outside that she didn't know about never mind.

My mother explained to her what it meant. I like that anecdote, which tells us much about those who grew up in palaces.

Rukiye *Sultan Efendi* was the paternal aunt of Neslişah *Sultan* and Hanzâde *Sultan* (grandchildren of the last Ottoman Sultan Vahdettin), who came and visit their aunt often. So we also knew them when we were children.

We would also like to hear about some memories of your guests.

When I was talking with my mother about our guests, I recalled an anecdote of Cemal Reşit Rey (a renowned Turkish composer), which he told to my paternal grandmother on one of his visits. "Ever since we were children, we were fond of music, for our mother was immersed in it. We had a grand piano, under which we were hiding to listen to our mother playing. Sometimes she would deliberately play wrong notes to see how we would react. I remember pleading: please mother, don't make the piano cry." I really liked his saying 'don't make the piano cry,' which I couldn't forget.

Calligrapher Hamid Aytaç used to teach my mother. He used to came once a week in the afternoon, and we used to have dinner together after the private calligraphy lesson. One day my mother offered him fruits after dessert, and he said: "Pardon me, but I can't have a cat shred a lion." Whenever they serve fruit after dessert, I pray for Hamid *Hodja*'s soul and tell this anecdote. Once he sent me a birthday card he signed, with my name specially penned by him as my father asked.

Hamid *Hodja* was treating us, children, well, spoiling us a little. Once, he delightfully fulfilled a wish of mine. I had asked if he could write the saying "Folly is free (therefore abundant)," which was famous among the children back then. So he wrote and signed it both in Latin and Arabic letters.

Photograph 31: Hamid Aytaç, while working.

Photograph 32: Esin Çelebi collection.

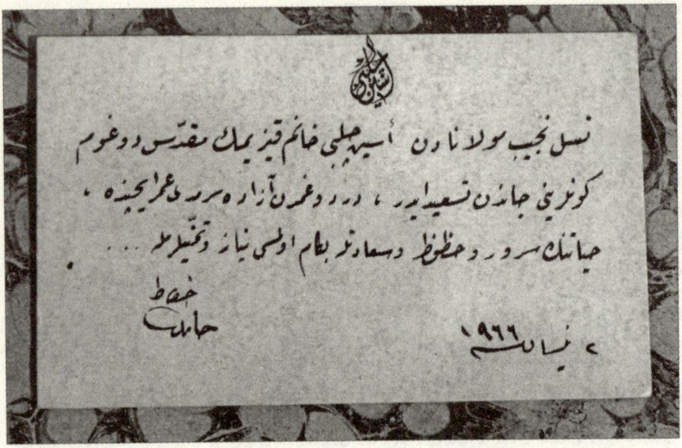

Photograph 33: The birthday card from Hamit *Hodja*.

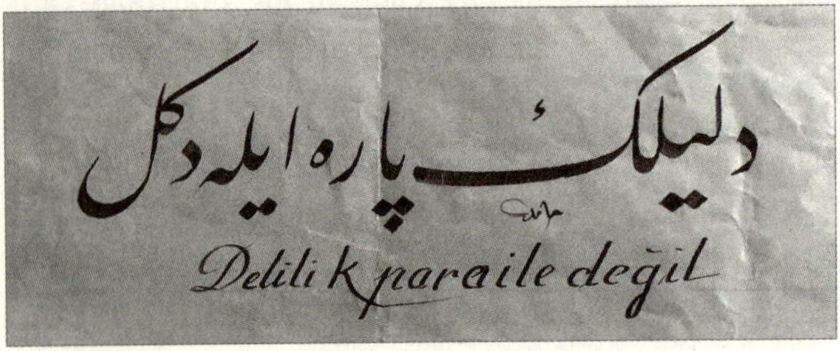

Photograph 34: "Folly is free (therefore abundant)."

Our dear Şefik Can *Hodja* taught Ottoman Turkish to us five siblings. When he received my wedding invitation, he sent me a congratulations letter in Ottoman script and a Quran as a gift.

We had a colorful childhood surrounded by beautiful people. We had the chance to be of service to them, which was something my father wanted and my mother permitted. They liked us to be the ones to serve the guests coffee, tea, and treats. Although we had housekeepers who were ready to help, they were kept from that. So we were catering to our guests, while the housekeepers were preparing everything to be served. In later years, my father was asking, "Daughter, bake a pie, bake a cake..." and it was my pleasure to grant his wish.

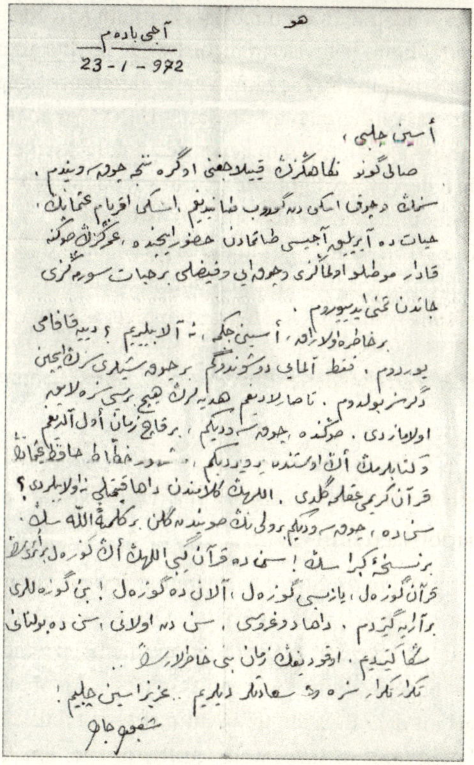

هو

آجی بادهم
23 - 1 - 972

أسين چلبی ،

صالی گونو نقاشلرك قيلاجغنی ادگره سنجه چوق سويندم .
سنك ده چوق اسكی ده گورب طانيديغم ، اسكی اقربام عثمانك
حيات ده آيريلوب آجيسی طاتمادن حضور ايچنده ، عمرلرك صوكنه
قادر موطلو اولمالرنی ده چوق ايی و فيضلی بر حيات سوره‌ركی
جانندن تمنی ايديورم .
برخاطره اولارق ، أسين چلبی ، نه آلابيليرم ؟ ديه قافامی
يورردم . فقط آلمايی دوشوندگم برچوق شيلری سزك ايچين
دگرسز بولدم . تا صاتلاديغم هديه لرك هيچ بريسی سزه لايق
اولامازدی . صوكنده چوق سودیگم ، برقاچ زمان اول آلديغم
[illegible] أك اوستنده بولنديغم ، شو [illegible] حافظ عثمان
قرآن كريمی عقلمه گلدی . اللهك كلامندن داها قيمتلی نه اولابيلردی ؟
سن ده ، چوق سودیگم [illegible] گلن بر كلمة الله سك .
برنسخهٔ كبرا سك ! سن ده قرآن گبی اللهك أك گوزل بر اثری
قرآن گوزل ، يازيسی گوزل ، آلان ده گوزل ! بو گوزللری
بر آرايه گتيردم . داها دوغروسی ، سن ده اولانی ، سن ده بولنانی
سكا گتيردم . اوقودقجه زمان بنی خاطرلارسك .
تكرار تكرار سزه ده سعادتلر ديلرم .. عزيز أسين چلبيم !
شفيق جان

Photograph 35: Şefik Can and his letter.

Hû

Acıbadem
23-1-972

Esin Çelebi,

Salı günü nikâhınızın kıyılacağını öğrenince çok sevindim. Sizin ve çok eskiden görüp tanıdığım eski akrabam Osman'ın hayatta ayrılık acısı tatmadan huzûr içinde, ömrünüzün sonuna kadar mutlu olmanızı ve çok iyi ve feyizli bir hayat sürmenizi candan temenni ediyorum.

Bir hâtıra olarak, Esinciğime ne alabilirim? diye kafamı yordum. Fakat almayı düşündüğüm birçok şeyleri sizin için değersiz buldum. Tasarladığım hediyelerin hiçbirisi size lâyık olamazdı. Sonunda, çok sevdiğim, birkaç zaman evvel aldığım ve kitaplarımın en üstünde yer verdiğim, meşhûr Hattât Hâfız Osman'ın Kurân-ı Kerîm'i aklıma geldi. Allah'ın kelâmından daha kıymetli ne olabilirdi? Sen de, çok sevdiğim bir velinin soyundan gelen bir kelimetullahsın. Bir nüsha-i kübrâsın! Sen de Kurân gibi Allah'ın en güzel bir eserisin. Kurân güzel, yazısı güzel, alan da güzel! Ben güzelleri bir araya getirdim. Daha doğrusu, senden olanı, sende bulunanı sana getirdim. Okuduğun zaman beni hatırlarsın.

Tekrar tekrar size saâdetler dilerim... azîz Esin Çelebim!

Şefik Can

Photograph 36: Turkish translation of a revised version of the letter (adapted to modern Turkish).

Esin Çelebi, *Hû*. I'm overjoyed to learn that you are getting married on Tuesday. I wish you and my relative Osman a peaceful, prosperous, blessed life together. May you always be happy and safe from any sorrow of separation. I've been thinking a lot about what I'm going to get my dear Esin for her wedding present. I had some ideas, although I felt none of them were worthy of you. Finally, the Quran, written in the calligraphy of the famous penman *Hâfız* Osman came to my mind. What could have been more precious than the words of Allah? Especially given that you, a descendant of a *wali* whom I dearly love, are a word of Allah. Just like the Quran, you are a great work of Allah, an exemplary creation of the Almighty. The Quran, its calligraphy work, and the recipient, are all beautiful. So I'm bringing together the beauties. Or more precisely, I brought you a reflection of what you already have inside. May you remember me as you read it. Again and many times, I wish you happiness... My beloved Esin Çelebi. Şefik Can Acıbadem 23-1-972

We had a colorful childhood surrounded by beautiful people. We had the chance to be of service to them, which was something my father wanted and my mother permitted. They liked us to be the ones to serve the guests coffee, tea, and treats. Although we had housekeepers who were ready to help, they were kept from that. So we were catering to our guests, while the housekeepers were preparing everything to be served. In later years, my father was asking, "Daughter, bake a pie, bake a cake..." and it was my pleasure to grant his wish.

Always serving, always catering to others...

Esin Çelebi: Yes, yes... Very fortunately. There's a saying: "Serving others is a path to find wisdom," it is absolutely true. We had our guests from abroad too. People who had interest in learning about Hz. Mevlânâ and the Mevlevî Order, including researchers like Anna Masala, Anne-Marie Schimmel, Eva de Vitray-Meyerovitch and more. Here we must also remember Fevzi Halıcı, who's done great services like the establishment of the Konya Tourism Association and its activities such as symposiums.

For example, the annual symposium held on May 3-5, which is the anniversary of the arrival of Hz. Mevlânâ and his family in Konya. My father, who got in touch with the president of Selçuk University Mr. Halil Cin, had brought the idea.

Namık Kemâl Zeybek, the Minister of Culture at the time, lent considerable support to these symposiums. He is still a treasured memory associated with my father. Talking about the Minister of Culture, I must also mention Agah Oktay Güner and Namık Kemal Zeybek, who were among my father's friends. May the other ones whom I skip mentioning give me their blessing.

In his later years, my father conducted valuable studies on *Masnavî* and *Dîvân-ı Kebîr*, working together with Şefik Can *Hodja* and Hüseyin Top *Dede*. Especially *Evrad-ı Sharif*, which my father prepared with Hüseyin Top *Dede*, is a very important reference for the history of the Mevlevî Order. Evrad-ı Sharif was written in dual script (Arabic-Latin) and a Latin translation. The book was also translated into Turkish, Persian, and German. Here I would like to thank everyone who contributed to that.

Burhan Öcal was another important personality in our lives. Everyone called him "Police *Brother*" and for us, he was "Polis *Efendi*." His father was a policeman, that's how he acquired the nickname. Police *Efendi* grew up in an orphanage, having survived meningitis in those years. There was a period when Yenikapı Mevlevî house was used as an orphanage. After the closure of the Mevlevî Houses, the building first became a primary school, and then remained idle for a while. And in Fahreddin Kerim Gökay's time, not only was the school re-opened, but the facility was also turned into an orphanage, offering street urchins a place to stay at night. After a while, the school was transferred to a more equipped facility, and the Mevlevî House remained as an orphanage. Police *Efendi* was working there - as janitor or nurse; I can't recall exactly. Just like our Mehmet Dede of Konya, Police *Efendi* didn't want to leave the place when he retired. So they employed him under a special status. He was different in a special way. Yenikapı owes him a lot, as he guarded the Mevlevî House at the risk of his life. He was a man of good manners, with a pure heart. May Allah bless him with heaven.

Every *Shab-i Arus,* Police *Efendi* traveled from Istanbul to visit us in Konya. There, he was assigned a duty, usually with the help of my father. He was always there, right next to the whirlers as if leading them, like: "Let's get on the bus now, it's time for lunch... Let's do this and that..." Everyone loved him dearly and tried to do as he said with a genuine effort. So, that is Burhan; I must certainly honor his place in my childhood memories. May Allah bless his soul.

You said, "In Fahreddin Kerim Gökay's time." Was it the municipality who re-opened the Mevlevî House for other uses?

In his time, the facility was turned into an orphanage to house street urchins. Today, Yenikapı Mevlevî House continues as Fatih Sultan Mehmet Foundation University, a center of knowledge and science.

Photograph 37: Yenikapı Mevlevî House.

Apparently, you grew up in a big family, in a crowded house. How are things today?

True. Today, although we live in different cities, we get together on every occasion. Especially, we gather around my mother Güzîde Çelebi each year on her birthday.

Photograph 38: Family photograph.

SERVICES/ACTIVITIES OF THE FOUNDATION

You are the vice-chairperson of the International Mevlânâ Foundation, spending considerable time there, serving under that roof. You seem to be the face of the foundation.

International Mevlânâ Foundation was established in 1996 upon my father's wish. The same year he passed away. Now we walk in the path he's set for us, in an effort to serve others. Faruk Hemdem Çelebi, my brother and my spiritual elder, has been the chairman of the foundation since its establishment. He's always been supported by our Mevlevî elders. In the beginning, I didn't have an official duty in the foundation. Two years after the establishment, my brother asked me to join. I immediately came on board when he said: "Sister, give me a hand in the foundation, let's work together. Your children are grown up, so you may spare time to serve here."

My position was an initiative of my siblings, especially of my brother Faruk Çelebi. Thinking it is better to have a spokesperson, they decided that I should be the one to assume a role in the forefront. My Çelebi assigned this duty to me.

Also, I believe my father offered me to Allah to be a person devoted to serving and helping others. I came to think of it because of my father's words (his prayer about me when I was a child), which I suddenly remembered many years later on a very busy day. When I was four, I had jaundice,

Photograph 39: Güzîde Çelebi and Celâleddin Çelebi together with their children

which turned so severe that it impacted my kidneys, and the resulting infection brought me in a serious condition. Under the circumstances of the time, it was decided to build a proper care unit at home. As the doctors said: "There's a medicine we can give via serum; that's all we can do to save her" my family accepted the treatment. They took me home and prepared my bed, which was basically our dining table covered with sheet.

My room had two doors, one that we regularly used, and one that remains closed; it was even covered with a curtain to block any noise. Behind the door was my father's study. It was much later, in my thirties, that I remembered something from these days, having sort of a flashback. I was looking down at myself from outside, from the top of that door. I was watching from a bright, spacious point. Observing my hands, my feet, grandma, my mother, the doctor lady, and our Armenian needler, whom we called Baron. They'd all lost hope... One by one, I was able to observe their places in the room.

When I mentioned that, my mother just said: "We'd been talking a lot. Maybe that's why." It was apparent; she didn't want to talk about that. Then one day, I asked my father: "I reminisced something like that, not sure what brought it back." He explained: "There, behind that door, I was praying to Allah: My Lord, please grant her life if my daughter will be a good person, worthy of her nation, her ancestors, her religion. Otherwise, she came from you; she is yours in any case." After that, he told me that my kidneys started to recover, and that is how I survived. Hearing these words from my father was something very profound of course. Then, years after his decease, one day, my father's words echoed in my mind. It was a hectic day, busy with the foundation's work. I was feeling exhausted. "My Lord, please grant her life if my daughter will be a good person, worthy of her nation, her ancestors, her religion." I realized that my father offered me to Allah to be a person of constant service. Praise be to Allah... May my Lord wrong me not, wrong us not, and make us all worthy of our blessed path.

Could you tell us about the mission and activities of the foundation?

As I mentioned earlier, at the time of the Law of Dervish Lodges, Atatürk invited Abdülhalim *Chalabi* to Ankara. And with their joint decision, Abdülhalim *Chalabi* appointed his son, my grandfather, as *sheikh* of the Aleppo Mevlevî House (which, among the others, was the closest to Turkey).

Preceding the stipulation of the Law of Dervish Lodges, Atatürk uttered the following words about the Mevlevî Order to Abdülhalim *Chalabi*, the Chief Master of Konya, and furthermore the Vice President of the First House of Representatives:

"You, the Mevlevîs have made a great difference by combating ignorance and religious fundamentalism for centuries, as well as making contributions to science and the arts. However, we are obliged not to make any exceptions and must include Mevlevî tekkes [in the closure of all the dervish lodges]. Nonetheless, the ideas and teaching of Mevlânâ will not only exist forever, but they will emerge even more powerfully in the future."

Today, the immense interest in Hz. Mevlânâ and the Mevlevî Order on a global scale proves Atatürk right. In light of his visionary words above, International Mevlânâ Foundation has been founded in Istanbul on March 10, 1996 with the spiritual support of our late father Celâleddin Bâkır Çelebi (Hz. Mevlânâ's 21st generation grandson), together with the family members and supporters including those who loved Hz. Mevlânâ.

The purpose of the foundation is to conduct research about the great Turkish Islamic thinker, scholar, and poet Mevlânâ Celâleddîn-i Rûmi, his works and thought and carry them over to the coming generations from all around the world. Therefore, it has become our mission and vision to conserve the Mevlevî culture and tradition, which has a history of nearly 800 years. Our activities are in many locations, both domestically and internationally.

As five siblings, we all carry the responsibility of being descendants of Hz. Mevlânâ. It is our lifetime mission to serve in his way and live up to his name. Our late father Celâleddin Bâkır Çelebi, May Allah bless his soul, offered great service in that respect. Meanwhile, our mother Güzîde

Çelebi, always stood by him. And now she is giving moral support to us.

Eflâkî *Dede*, in his work *Manaqib al-Ârifin* quotes these significant words of Hz. Mevlânâ: "By Allah, by Allah! The meaning (of the words of the Masnavî) will take hold and extend from the rising place of the sun to where it sets, and it will travel to (all) the climates (of the world). And there will not be any meeting or gathering where these words will not be recited--to the extent that they will be read (out loud) in places of worship and on benches. And all religious communities will wear a garment (consisting) of those words."[10]

So, the International Mevlânâ Foundation was established upon the wish of my father, Celâleddin Bâkır Çelebi. Today, my brother and spiritual elder Faruk Hemdem Çelebi is the chairman; and I serve as the vice-chairperson. Among the foundation's main activities, there are national and international conferences, symposiums, workshops held on the life and works Hz. Mevlânâ, his teachings, the Mevlevî tradition as well as topics like *semâ*. We cooperate with government institutions, civil society institutions, as well as experts from academia and the Mevlevî tradition.

Photograph 40: The Logo of the International Mevlânâ Foundation.

10 Translator's Note: English translation by Ibrahim Gamard from the original work in Persian (Eflâki, Manâqibu 'l`ârifîn, 3/427) is taken from: http://www.dar-al-Masnavi.org/rumi-on-Masnavi.html#67.

Our board of trustees has 57 members, including not only some descendants of Hz. Mevlânâ, but also other supporters who contribute through their scholarly work or other forms of service.

Our executive board has nine members, elected semiannually from among the board of trustees. The executive board meeting every month is responsible for the overall management, carrying out the activities, and proposing new projects as necessary. Meanwhile, the board of trustees provides support and guidance through their working groups and task forces in their specific fields.

So, your father Celâleddin Bâkır Çelebi offered great service, spearheading the foundation's establishment and activities.

My father passed his business responsibilities in commerce and agriculture to my brother Faruk Hemdem Çelebi as soon as he finished school. That was to detach himself from worldly concerns, to dedicate his life to serving Hz. Mevlânâ and the Mevlevî culture, spreading his knowledge all around the world. With remarkable enthusiasm, he accepted all invitations to join meetings, never passing up an opportunity. He delivered speeches on the Mevlevî manners and path in Pakistan, Jordan, Tunisia, Cyprus, Greece, France, Spain, Germany, Austria, Poland, Italy, Sweden, Norway, and the United States. The whirlers and musicians who accompanied my father on these travels also helped the promotion of the Mevlevî culture in many different ways. In 1989, during the General Conference of UNESCO in Paris, my father gave a speech on Hz. Mevlânâ and love. Following his suggestions and with the institution's internal vote, UNESCO proclaimed 1990 as "The International

Year of Love." As a polyglot, Çelebi addressed people in their own languages in most of his international speeches. And there were times the audience expressed their admiration for our culture. That's when my father was happiest of all.

For instance, the Austrian Minister of Culture made the following remarks in a conference held there: *"Centuries ago, your ancestors had set out to conquer our land. Now you are achieving what they failed to do back then. Today you are making a cultural conquest. I offer my heartfelt thanks to Celâleddin Çelebi for enriching us with the knowledge of the Turkish culture, and for passing on messages of friendship from Hz. Mevlânâ. I would also like to express my admiration for the Turkish culture."* After the speech in Pakistan, one of the jubilant listeners cheered, *"Turks, who bowed down to no one, would be the only rightful leader of the Muslim world. I thank Çelebi for his speech."* I must also mention the speeches, on the unity of religions, in Italy and Spain, where my father addressed priests. Also, his speech on peace, unity, and solidarity in Sweden, which led to the welcoming of many Bosnian refugees. My father deemed it to be cultural service when *semâ* performances and his speeches were broadcast on TV in the countries he visited. Steering clear of pride and vanity, he dedicated himself to serving others.

Celâleddin Çelebi had been an invited speaker at many events of non-governmental organizations. There were also annual, periodic events, including the *Shab-i Arus* Commemorations, Annual Hz. Mevlânâ Congresses held by Konya Selçuk University in May, and the Istanbul Festival organized by the Istanbul Foundation for Culture and Arts (İKSV). Besides these, the Rose Festivals and the Food Congresses were the occasions to gather with friends.

Whether for hundreds of people or only a single person, on every occasion, Çelebi spoke of Hz. Mevlânâ, of love, unity, and solidarity. He generously shared his knowledge and compassion with everyone. He touched thirsty hearts and souls with anecdotes from Hz. Mevlânâ, introducing them to the great Turkish Sufi. In 1989, in recognition of these efforts, he was awarded an honorary doctorate by Konya Selçuk University that was presented by the University's President Halil Cin, which my father humbly accepted as a spiritual reward.

The foundation's headquarters in Konya is adjacent to the Hz. Mevlânâ Museum and Tomb. Had this place formerly been the first Mevlevî House?

Hz. Mevlânâ's tomb had formerly been the rose garden of the Seljuk Sultan Alaaddin Keykubat. Once, on a spring day, Hz. Mevlânâ and his father went on an excursion, visiting the garden. As Hz. Mevlânâ's father, the Sultan of Scholars, liked the place, Alaaddin Keykubat granted it as a gift to him. Shortly after that, Hz. Mevlânâ's father walked to *Haqq*. He became the first to be buried in the garden, upon Sultan Alaaddin's proposal to the family: "Let's make two good things happen at once." Later, this was followed by other family members, and then Hz. Mevlânâ, who was buried next to his father.

At the time, the dervish lodge was not in place?

There was nothing. Hz. Mevlânâ didn't establish a religious order. He taught at *madrasas* and held religious conversations. After he walked to Haqq, his disciples wanted to build a dome above his tomb. So the green dome (*kubba-i hadrâ*) in Hz. Mevlânâ's Tomb was erected on four big pillars back then. Several changes were made over time, including the construction of the surrounding walls to convert the space into an enclosed area. When his father passed away, Hz. Mevlânâ's disciples had asked if they could build a shrine. Hz. Mevlânâ had objected: "Can you build any better dome, anything more magnificent than the sky?"

Nevertheless, his disciples built Hz. Mevlânâ's tomb. Later, the first Mevlevî House (what we know today as Mevlânâ Museum) was built around the shrine, making the place a building complex with sections like *semâhâne* (whirling hall), *masjid* (prayer room) and rooms for the Mevlevî elders.

All these were renovated as of today. The Madrasa of Sultan Veled, a boarding school for the disciples, was originally in the front section of the complex. However, it was demolished in time, and so was a *hammam* (traditional public bath).

We understand that your family was running the hammam, which was then demolished for some reason.

Well, the family established the Celaliye Foundation, which had many properties in the Ottoman times. However, all its possessions, including the *hammam,*were confiscated by the government per the Law of Dervish Lodges. In any case, my family never had an income from that *hammam*. Because, as I mentioned, my grandfather was sent to Aleppo just before the enactment of the Law of Dervish Lodges. My father and we were born there.

In their earlier times at Konya, both Hz. Mevlânâ and his father taught at the İplikçi Madrasa, which was an important educational institution in Anatolia at Seljuk times. It was once a major building complex with the school and the mosque, from which only the mosque survives until today.

The madrasas were religious schools. Hz. Mevlânâ had a profound knowledge of the Quran, but he made a living just from teaching.

When was the first Mevlevî House built?

The first Mevlevî House was built by Hz. Mevlânâ's son Sultan Veled and his grandson Ulu Arif Chalabi in order to pass on Hz. Pir's teachings to future generations. This initial House in Konya became the central point, trained disciples and sent them over to other cities. This gradually formed the network of Mevlevî Houses (including "*âsitâne*"s and smaller "*zâviye*"*s*), which expanded in line with the growth trajectory of the Ottoman Empire.

How were the Mevlevî Houses managed?

The management of the Mevlevî Houses was always central. All the sheikhs were appointed from one point. Ever since its establishment, the Mevlevî Order has been presided over by a Chief Master (*Maqam Chalabi)* elected from among Mevlânâ's offspring from the side of his son Sultan Veled. Sultan Veled and Ulu Arif Chalabi aimed to conserve Hz. Mevlânâ's teachings by putting all the knowledge in a framework. In a way, they established a school of thought.

Chief Masters, always from Hz. Mevlânâ's bloodline, also had to be knowledgeable and equipped with the management skills required by their duty. As the historical records show, the lineage of Chief Masters originates from Hz. Mevlânâ's son Sultan Veled, and continues today without interruption. Until the Law of Dervish Lodges, Konya was the central location where the Chief Masters dwelled. After that, Aleppo became the new center.

Photograph 41: Abdülhalim Çelebi, Mehmed Bâkır Çelebi and Celâleddin Bâkır Çelebi.

Do we still have these records today?

Yes, these are kept in the archive of the Mevlânâ Museum in Konya. The records are up to date, so they include the names of my brother Faruk Hemdem Çelebi and my father Celâleddin Bâkır Çelebi. When we were asked: "How do you know you are the 22nd generation grandchildren of Hz. Mevlânâ?" We respond: "A historical record of the family tree, which had been kept over the years, is in the Mevlânâ Museum in Konya.

Could you tell us more about the activities of the foundation?

The foundation aims to promote and disseminate the thought and teachings of Hz. Mevlânâ, who is from the heart of our culture, and at the same time a prominent historical figure who belonged to humanity. For that matter, the foundation has carried out local and international activities since its establishment in 1996. The Mevlevî culture is based on eight hundred years of tradition. In that respect, the foundation took solid steps by obtaining the necessary international accreditations to preserve this cultural heritage in its authenticity for future generations.

The International Year of Rumi (announced by UNESCO) was among the foundation's works.

The foundation undertook all the necessary preparations, including the files for Turkey's formal application via the Ministry of Culture and Tourism. Consequently, UNESCO proclaimed the Mevlevî Sema Ceremony as a Masterpiece of the Oral and Intangible Heritage of Humanity and declared 2007 to be the International Year of Mevlânâ Celâleddîn Rûmî for it was the 800th anniversary of his birth. In the meantime, the International Mevlânâ Foundation has become the only accredited institution by UNESCO in the field of Hz. Mevlânâ and the Mevlevî Order.

We had begun the process by working on a project initiated by UNESCO. The institution first accepted submissions from all over the world on candidates to be nominated as the oral and intangible cultural heritage of humanity.

In that respect, we prepared the file to nominate "Semâ and the Mevlevî Music" for its recognition and conservation as cultural heritage, working in cooperation with a group of esteemed friends and expert practitioners who came from the tradition, and the academicians who conduct research in the field. In each country, the project files were first prepared by the relevant non-governmental organizations, then submitted for review and approval to the Ministry of Culture, which then applied to UNESCO.

Our file consisted of many sub-sections on the Mevlevî Order. Hence, for three years, we worked with UNESCO to address the institution's various questions on the topic. As per UNESCO's decision announced under the headline "Social Practices, Rituals, and Festive Events" in November 2005, the Mevlevî semâ ceremony was included in "The Representative List of the Intangible Cultural Heritage of Humanity," marking its official place in the modern global culture. This is a landmark achievement. The official letter from UNESCO said: "Your government has some good news to share with the public." The Ministry of Culture signed a contract with UNESCO. Although the project is initiated by us, the Ministry is the official body to preserve the cultural heritage. However, we received a letter instructing us to supervise the work of Ministry as necessary. We cooperated with the Ministry in many projects, some ongoing. The project's primary documents, including technical details, was published in the Turkish/English bilingual book "Yüzyıllar Boyu Mevlânâ ve Mevlevîlik / Mevlânâ and Mevlevî Order Throughout Centuries"[11] thanks to the cooperation of the Ministry of Culture and the support of Turkcell. Here I would like to thank everyone who contributed to this book, of which I was the editor.

---

11 Bayru, Esin Çelebi (ed.), *Yüzyıllar Boyu Mevlânâ ve Mevlevîlik / Mevlânâ and Mevlevî Order Throughout Centuries*, Kültür ve Turizm Bakanlığı Yayınları, İstanbul, 2008.

Right after this process, again with the approval of the Ministry of Culture, we prepared and submitted our project "Hz. Mevlânâ's 800th Birthday" to UNESCO. The Year of Mevlânâ Celâleddîn-i Rûmî was celebrated both nationally and internationally with many festive events.

Can you elaborate on the accreditation?

After evaluation of our work, in its Paris Meeting, UNESCO declared the accreditation of the International Mevlânâ Foundation as the sole non-governmental institution to be recognized in the field of the Mevlevî culture. Therefore, since 2014, Turkey has been represented in UNESCO by Mr. Işın Çelebi, a trustee of our foundation.

The third lasting project of the foundation was undertaken in 2014 with the aim of proper communication and representation of Mevlânâ and the Mevlevî culture. In that respect, the foundation obtained registrations from the Turkish Patent and Trademark Office on the names and words defining the terminology of Hz. Mevlânâ and the Mevlevî culture, placing them under the protection of the government.

We have also collaborated with the Ministry of Culture on the project "Istanbul 2010 European Capital of Culture". We organized weekly semâ ceremonies, monthly meetings, and concerts in the Yenikapı Mevlevî House from June to December that year. We also organized events in cooperation with the Municipality for the project "Konya: Capital of Islamic Culture for 2016".

We conceive all our initiatives with a global mindset. With invitations from all around the world, we are working to promote Hz. Mevlânâ and the Mevlevî culture.

You collaborate with government institutions on many projects.

For all our initiatives, we cooperated with the Ministry of Culture, directly or through its representative office in Konya. We have always viewed them as our project partners. The same holds for the Municipality of Konya. We consistently obtain government approval or some form of official support for our initiatives, which we deem very important in terms of preventing any misunderstandings. Establishment of the Selçuk University Mevlânâ Institute, which I serve as an advisor, a closely engaged partner of the foundation, was something my late father dearly wished for but didn't live to see. Besides collaborating with government institutions, municipalities, and non-governmental organizations, the International Mevlânâ Foundation works with a community of experts, including scientists, researchers, writers, and people from the tradition.

We also provide guidance, know-how, and moral support to the associations abroad that work on Hz. Mevlânâ, some of which are in the United States, Switzerland, Germany, Holland, and Iran.

We understand that you have moved to Konya in order to focus more on the foundation's activities

If I may, I would like to say a few words about the times preceding my relocation. Until 2011, we had been to Konya at least three times every year, the first one being May 3-5, the anniversary of Hz. Mevlânâ and his family's arrival to Konya. On these dates, Selçuk University organized national and internal symposiums, where my father used to participate as a keynote speaker. The symposiums resulted from the joint efforts of him, Mr. Namık Kemal Zeybek, the Minister of Culture of the Time, and Mr. Halil Cin, the President of Selçuk University.

The other two dates when we regularly visited Konya was September 30th, Hz. Mevlânâ's birthday and the week of December 17th. We have always spent these times in Konya. There were other occasional visits too. We wanted to be in Konya, where our hearts lie.

In between those back-and-forth visits, our friends proposed, "Why don't you stay here and open a branch for the foundation?" With the approval of the board of trustees, the

Photograph 42: Opening of the Konya Branch of the Foundation on May 3, 2011.

Pictured (from left to right): Canan Sayar, Neslipir Çelebi Sayar, Tahir Akyürek (Mayor of Konya), Esin Çelebi Bayru, Hatice Doğan, Ayşe Türkmenoğlu (MP for Konya), Aydın Nezih Doğan (Governor of Konya), Mustafa Çıpan (Provincial Director of Culture), Mehmet Hançerli (Mayor of Karatay).

Foundation's branch in Konya was opened on May 3, 2011. Here, we work with Nadir Karnıbüyükler (the president of the Konya branch), Fahri Özçakıl, Mehmet Emin Holat, and Sami Küçük.

Here I must also mention, Assoc. Prof. Nuri Şimşekler, the founding President of Selçuk University Mevlânâ Institute, who made significant contributions to our foundation. May Allah be pleased with him.

When I started to work in the Konya branch, my husband Osman Bayru suggested, "My dear wife, it's not like you'll be able to return from Konya; we'd better move there." That's how we moved in 2015. Now we are quite happy to live here.

I am deeply grateful to my husband. Being the grandson of Sheikh Osman Efendi, the sheikh of the Yenikapı Mevlevî House, he has a very good understanding of my spiritual duties and responsibilities. This makes my efforts a lot easier. Konya embraced him as its *enişte* (husband of the sister). Everyone from the governor to the janitor refers to him in that way.

What would you like to tell us about Konya? Do the people here appreciate Hz. Mevlânâ?

Konya had historically been an important city even before the arrival of Hz. Mevlânâ. Hz. Pîr was in his 20s when he arrived here to spend the rest of his life. Although there were times he traveled to Damascus, Konya was his hometown. Ever since then, the city has been associated with Hz. Mevlânâ. Those who know him come to know Konya, come to know Turkey. We must be aware that Hz. Mevlânâ plays an important role in the promotion of our country. It is a great honor for us. The people of Konya should have a deep understanding of Hz. Mevlânâ, who teaches us so well about divine love. We need to grasp that serving Hz. Mevlânâ means serving humanity. The people of Konya, who don't do much to read and learn about the matter, are unaware of the cultural and spiritual importance of the treasure that the city houses. Believe it or not, we happen to learn things that we don't know about Hz. Mevlânâ from some of the foreign visitors in Konya, with whom we exchange our knowledge too.

This year the Chinese were among the top in terms of the number of visitors. They had been taught well about the manners of visiting the place. In the heat of the summer, they entered the shrine by covering their heads and shoulders, they knew where to step and stand; they are not even Muslims. The visitors to the shrine need to be mindful of their steps and voices, avoiding any noise so as not to disturb the others who pray in the sacred place. Also, the guides and the officers working in the place must have the necessary training, so that they know and tell others that it is a matter of good manners.

"Hz. Mevlânâ Celâleddîn-i Rûmî Culture Village"

Today, inevitably, we need to build the proper means to address the rising global interest in Hz. Mevlânâ and the Mevlevî culture. In light of this notion, I would like to mention another important project: "Hz. Mevlânâ Celâleddîn-i Rûmî Culture Village", which resulted from the considerable efforts of the International Mevlânâ Foundation over the years.

Our main goal is to safeguard the Mevlevî culture and tradition, the legacy of our ancestors, and pass it on to future generations in its authentic form. That is the primary concern of the foundation's activities. What may be the cornerstones of our culture face the risk of degeneration today. Yet, as it has become evident, these teachings benefit the whole world.

The "village" project was my childhood dream. In those years, we were having guests from all over the world, people who love Hz. Mevlânâ. Especially the ones from the Europe asked, "We want to learn, who can teach us?" There were no formal schools anymore as the Mevlevî Houses were closed since the Law of Dervish Lodges in 1925. However, all the classes that were once taught at the Mevlevî Houses were then held in the universities.

As I often heard the question "Where can we get an education?", I was envisioning a school back then. But my vision was an open school that would accept people without pre-requisites like diplomas, offering a variety of courses and classes. In time, this vision has evolved into the "village" idea as it is today. I wish we could have a traditional Konya neighborhood from the 13th century in the village. And it is probably a better idea to build the village in the outskirts of the city. I hope the village will attract people from all around the world. All the classes that were taught in the Mevlevî Houses should be available both in English and Turkish, open to everyone who is interested.

For the village project, we have received a lot of invitations from abroad as well, like the United States and India. But I think we should first open the village in Konya. To me, this is both a personal dream and a professional endeavor. Those who will make it happen should have the relevant capacity.

I think the government's involvement is especially important. When the Law of Dervish Lodges was enacted, all the Mevlevî Houses and their possessions passed into the ownership of the General Directorate for Foundations. Therefore I think the government has the means to support the project. In the end, the village will serve the promotion of Turkish culture. People do need that kind of an open university, where they have opportunities to learn and share in spiritual development.

The project also needs support on the side of the local authorities. For that matter, we have registered the "village" as the culture project in the Konya Plains Project, which is a success. However, we need further support from the municipalities, such as assignment of land, engagement in the project feasibility studies and architectural works. I hope we can partner with the Ministry of Culture and Tourism, and the Ministry of Development but keeping it open-to-all is of utmost importance. We can build an online platform where people can remotely search and register for the classes. Although the project is an initiative of the foundation, we would like to welcome all those who are willing to support it.

Hopefully, we will make it. I hope and believe that we can build it first in Konya, then all around the world. It is much needed. In my experience so far, based on the events I attended abroad, I've seen venues -located a little ways out-of-town-, which could be used for a variety of occasions. I think we need a center like that. I said everything I had to say. From here on, it's all up to the government leaders; we hope to get this project off the ground with their support. And I repeat, the whole world needs it.

In a nutshell, how can you define the discipline of Mevlevî Order?

The discipline of Mevlevî Order was established by Hz. Mevlânâ's son Sultan Veled and grandson Ulu Arif Chalabi, with the aim of passing on Hz. Mevlânâ's teachings to future generations. Over many centuries, it has proven to be a school, a path leading to "human maturity," enlightening people not just in Anatolia but in the Balkans, Asia, Africa, the Arab States, and today extending its outreach to all regions in the world - including the United States and Australia.

How was the education in the Mevlevî Houses?

Mevlevî Houses have always served as sort of conservatories or art academies while giving education on Hz. Mevlânâ's teachings along with theology, literature, and philology (Arabic and Persian languages).

A young aspirant who applied to a Mevlevî House had to be a decent person who had reached the age of majority, and who had the approval of his parents. The candidates lacking their parents' consent were rejected and sent back to obtain it.

After all, it was a life-changing decision. Once the candidate met these pre-requisites, he would be taken to the *matbâh-ı sharif* (kitchen) for three days, to be seated in a designated place to observe the way of life in the Mevlevî House. He was given food and water, but no one spoke to him so as to avoid any influence. During this time, he would be observed by the elder dervishes *(dede)* who measured his patience and his general state. The elders were good judges of character, they could tell by the look whether the candidate was fit or not. If they deemed him to be unfit, they would turn the tips of his shoes towards the door, signaling kindly a request for him to leave. It was also possible that the candidate could leave, in case of a change of heart, no questions asked. An accepted candidate was allowed to spend 18 days in his own clothes, so that he could be free to leave if he wishes.

However, if he decided to stay, he would be led to Sheikh Efendi by an elder, either the chief of the kitchen or the dede who is in charge of the general organization of the dervish lodge. *Sheikh Efendi*, after consulting with the elder, submitted the candidate to a *dede.* So the candidate would begin an education under the guidance of this "advisory teacher," first learning to read and write in case he was illiterate, then moving on to learning languages (Ottoman, Arabic, Persian) and the Quran. The curriculum also included reading and comprehension of Hz. Mevlânâ's works, and many courses that were taught in divinity schools. In that respect, the Mevlevî Houses functioned like faculties of theology and literature. There were also music classes. Depending on his aptitude, a student could learn to play an instrument. Otherwise, the education aimed to refine his ear for music. In any case, music was taught to all, because a musician must know of *semâ*, and a *semâzen* must know of music in order to achieve harmony. In accordance with his skills, a student could also take classes in the traditional arts, such as calligraphy, tezhip (ornamentation), or miniature painting. The training, which lasted 1001 days, included many of the courses that would have been taught in a conservatory, an academy, or a divinity school.

That meant a multifaceted tutelage, educating the disciples physically, spiritually, and knowledge-wise. We can think of a Mevlevî House as a boarding school, but one without a janitor. As part of their training, the students were to run errands in 18 different chores. These included the following: kitchen work, bed-making, bathroom hygiene, and shopping. In that schooling of self-discipline, a student could suddenly find himself cleaning the toilets the moment he started to think "he is somebody."

He was also put to tests for assessment of his attitude and personality. For example, he was given a shopping list and some money, was ordered to "go and fetch what's in the list!" It was then observed: if he spent idle time, hung around or returned as soon as he performed the duty, whether he picked and chose the vegetables, made the best use of money or not. These are all important necessities in a person's upbringing.

The *dede* who supervised the student assigned him whatever classes he deemed necessary for the student's spiritual disciplining. When it comes to *semâ*, it is also a teaching of this school. Today there are people who visit the foundation and say, "We would like to learn *semâ,*" but learning *semâ* comes with many other pre-requisites...

According to what my paternal grandmother told, a "dervish chest," inspired by the traditional *dowry chest,* was prepared by the women in *harem* for the dervishes who completed their period of tests. Everything from clothes, underwear, to ritual gowns were all sewn by hand and placed in the chest. These were not sold in the bazaars in those times.

Refined manners and rules of conduct (âdap ve erkân) are very important aspects of the Mevlevî tradition. States like politeness, purity, grace are sought. The etiquette of eating,

drinking, walking, sitting, standing up, speaking, and even relationships with the non-living things reflect manners of courtesy. There are quite a number of rules and conventions in the Mevlevî tradition. What could be the reason for that? Can we say that such kind of diversity and depth is the accumulation of eight hundred centuries? On the other hand, symbolism has also a special place in the Mevlevî tradition. What would you like to tell about that?

It is, of course, true that certain acts of Hz. Pîr were later adopted as rituals. However, Mevlevî Houses are like boarding schools, which must have a set of rules, which require discipline. A disciple there must know of the modes of conduct and discipline of living together. Today people act in their own way. "I am free!" is their statement of excuse. Yet freedom is not without boundaries. If I transgress the limits of my personal freedom, I disturb others, violating their rights.

A lesson that I had from Hz. Pîr is my piece of advice for everyone: "First you shall know yourself," which is something that our religion also tells. Knowledge of the self makes one aware of how valuable it is to be a human, how my Lord created us human beings as the most honorable of all creatures. When we conceive this phenomenon, we begin to love ourselves. "To know" is the first condition, "to love" is the second. Therefore, we must start with ourselves. All these rituals are intended to reveal this message. If we know and love ourselves, then we can share this love with others around us. Mevlevî dervishes greet each other by kissing the back of each other's hands at the same time. Age and status don't matter here. It could be that a ten-year-old greets a ninety-year-old, or a sheikh greets a novice; they kiss each other's hands. This has a very beautiful meaning: all souls are equal, there's no superiority among them.

The Mevlevî Houses no longer provide schooling, but we still have the opportunity to adopt some of their ways and methods.

This is what we have learned from our elders. Living by these rules would not only bless us with peace but also make us bring peace to others. It deeply impresses people when they hear about this particular way of greeting. Or, the gesture of inclining one's head while placing the hand over heart is as if it means "you are in my heart." As a symbolic token of amity, unity, peace. These are what humanity seeks today. Each and every gesture in the Mevlevî system bears such a beautiful symbolic meaning that once you know about their essence, you feel like using them.

You organize an event under the name "Şerbet-i Velâdet," can you tell us about that?

"Şerbet-i Velâdet" is organized annually on September 30th to celebrate the birth anniversary of Hz. Mevlânâ. The event takes place on the Mengüç Street, a neighborhood with the old houses rehabilitated by the Konya Municipality in 2015. The ceremony begins with the prayer at the Tomb of Hz. Mevlânâ, then the participants walk to the Mengüç street, where a cauldron containing *şerbet* (traditional sweet drink) is opened with prayers, and the attendants are served. We are trying to build a tradition together with the craftsmen of Konya, who support this public event with the complimentary treats they cater on a voluntary basis. With all these, it becomes a beautiful, joyous celebration.

Photograph 43: Prayer in front of the Cauldron of Şerbet.

Pictured: Yakup Canbolat (Governor of Konya), Şükrü Yaman (Konya Provincial Police Chef), Abdüssettar Yarar (Konya Provincial Director of Culture), Esin Çelebi Bayru, Sheikh Nadir Karlıbüyükler, Sheikh Fahri Özçakıl, Yıldırım Ekin (Mevlevî Sheikh from Holland), İbrahim Gamard (Mevlevî Sheikh from the United States), Anne Regard Cunz, Hikmet Çetiner, Nurullah Urvasızoğlu.

You also have a project for honoring the memory of the Karaman-Konya journey of Hz. Mevlânâ and his family.

Yes, we have a project for organizing a march from Karaman to Konya. As known, Hz. Mevlânâ and his family headed towards Anatolia after they left Balkh and completed their pilgrimage in Mecca-Medina. After sojourning in a number of Anatolian cities, the family arrived to Karaman, where they lived for about seven years and eventually moved to

Konya upon the invitation of the Seljuk Sultan Alaaddin Keykubat.

I used to wonder and imagine about the path of their journey, the places they visited.

We initiated a project in order to revive this memory so that people would embark on a spiritual journey and, at the same time, walk for the sake of engaging in physical activity. First, national and international symposiums were held at Selçuk University for the commemoration of the anniversary of the arrival of Hz. Mevlânâ and his family to Konya. Since 2007, their departure from Karaman and arrival to Konya on May 3rd have been celebrated with representative ceremonies. In 2016, with regard to Hz. Mevlânâ's teachings, we have initiated "The International Love and Peace March." The march begins on April 27 in Karaman, with the prayer at the tomb of Hz. Mevlânâ's mother Mümine *Hatun*, and ends on May 3rd with the prayer at the tomb of Hz. Mevlânâ in Konya. The participants stay in the towns and villages along their path, take part in the evening activities involving music and conversations. I believe that in the forthcoming years, we will observe a larger turnout with participants from all around the world. Governorships of Karaman and Konya, Provincial Directorates of Culture, and Municipalities partnered with us on this project; we would like to express our gratitude to them and especially to Konya AFAD (Disaster and Emergency Management Presidency).

Do you also participate in the march?

I can't say I walk all the way, but rather participate to the extent I can walk. In the meantime, I'm in charge of the organization. Our march begins, with the participation of the Governor of Karaman and his protocol, after the prayer in Aktekke, where the tomb of Hz. Mevlânâ's mother is located. Every year the governor, the mayor, and the protocol march with us for a distance of 4-5 kilometers. During this pleasant walk, we also find the opportunity to engage in pleasant conversations. We talk about Hz. Mevlânâ and the Mevlevî tradition in the places we visit along our path, and at night we stay in tents. Our activity is open to everyone.

Photograph 44: On the march (May 3, 2018).

Pictured: Yakup Canbolat (Governor of Konya), Abdüssettar Yarar (Konya Provincial Director of Culture), Esin Çelebi Bayru, Firuzande Erbabi, Fahri Özçakıl.

Hz. Mevlânâ's family arrived in Konya on May 3rd; therefore we plan our march around this date of arrival. First year the march took five days, the second year seven days... We received requests for spreading it over a longer time period, walking shorter laps with more breaks and more conversations.

Güzîde Çelebi: It was something (Celâleddin) Çelebi dearly wished. It's like we obligated the people of Konya to hold ceremonies on May 3rd-5th, September 30th, and December 17th, as we traveled to Konya every year on these dates. Given the tourists attracted, the community here held on to it, paving the way for traditionalising these events. There were many who wished yet couldn't come to join and watch the ritual here in the winter due to adverse weather or some other reasons. Thanks to the various projects and events organized by the Foundation on these three different time periods, crowds from all around the world get to visit Konya both at the end of September, in the beginning of May and in December. Thank Allah a thousand of times. The visitors have the opportunity to learn and see.

Can you tell us about other forthcoming projects of the foundation?

There are several projects. I would like to mention an initiative about children. Thankfully there was no television in our times; our paternal grandmother used to tell us tales. Then we grew up and noticed that she raised us with the stories from the Mesnevî, where each and every tale is so beautiful. We now have a related ongoing project for the children, which we named "My Mevlânâ," and launched three years ago with the joint efforts of the Ministry of National Education.

We work on a set of questions, including: how could children learn about Hz. Mevlânâ, how best could they understand him, what do they expect from us? We work on these questions together with the children and answer their questions. In that respect, several drama pieces were prepared for the children to perform on stage; the pieces are available to share with the public upon request. There are also songs, which we presented and obtained approval from the Ministry of National Education. These works contain information that promotes Turkish tradition, our own culture. This project started in Konya.

We also share this knowledge with teachers visiting from other cities. Hz. Mevlânâ bestowed on us a view of life, an exemplary lifestyle. That vision of life, I believe, is meant to enrich the world with a different perspective. As you know, Hz. Mevlânâ's time was a challenging period too. Like today, people in those times lacked hope, feeling helpless, crestfallen. In the meantime, I think Hz. Pîr's words transcend time. His words are still current. And his works, translated to many different languages across the globe, keep reaching the masses today.

Do you think the foundation receives good support and interest from the public and the authorities?

What can I say? No. It is a heartbreaking question indeed. We are trying to sustain the foundation with our own efforts and resources. When it comes to the level of interest, a majority of our guests are visitors from abroad, who generally prefer to research about us and the Mevlevî culture on available sources like the internet before their visit.

What is your view of the Mevlevî reciprocations performed at various places?

As you know, prior to the Law of Dervish Lodges semâ rituals were performed in the Mevlevî Houses, especially during *Shab-i Arus*. *Semâ* was performed in all conscience on Thursday nights, on the eve of religions holidays, at worshiping nights (*ihyâ geceleri*). Sometimes the ritual was initiated when the dervishes, in ecstasy of divine love, asked *Meydancı Dede*, who in turn asked for permission of *Sheikh Efendi*; the ceremony started after the *sheikh*'s sheepskin was brought to the *semâ* hall/ while calling out *"semâya selâ"* (call to semâ).

But now we see, at inappropriate places, performances what I may call as "the act of revolving"- for I'm unable to bring myself to call it "*semâ*." I find it hurtful when this whirling takes place in the guise of a dervish.

Revolving is a natural motion for humans; whirling is an expression of the soul's ecstasy, but it requires decency. Before wearing his clothes for *semâ*, a *semâzen* always fulfilled his religious duties: he performed ablution and salat of the time and prepared himself for *dhikr* (remembrance of Allah). Only then he could dress up, again with prayers, in his ritual robes and the other *semâ* clothes, and only then he could step on the *meydân-ı sharif*. We react strongly to what we see today. It is obvious that *semâ* and tasawwuf music must be taken under protection. Concerning that issue, which is unsettling for everyone and even more so for us, we prepared a case and presented the file to the Ministry of Culture.

Speaking of which, could you tell us about the foundation's initiative on "Semâ"?

Well, our project was named "Preservation of Semâ and Mevlevî Music," and it featured various subsections on other matters about the Mevlevî Order. We carry on our efforts under the protection of the government. Whenever there is a change of duty, we remind the new Minister of Culture of the project. Until today the Ministry of Culture issued three motions concerning the matter. By nature, these notes lack any power of sanction, but they do relay a disapproving message: “Don’t do this, it is not right,” and also contain a written guideline as to what kind of places are appropriate for *semâ.* Nurturing awareness is more effective than imposing bans. I believe people would come to respect and avoid performing this ritual in the wrong places, if we could inform and educate them on good practices and the cultural sensitivities involved. Also, this situation tells us that we must work further. Hopefully, people will grow conscious of the spiritual essence of what they are doing, and this underlying spirit will eventually set them on the right path.

Photograph 45: Semâ ritual in the yard of Hz. Mevlânâ’s tomb.

We hope so, too. What would you like to say about semâ?

In the words of my father Celâleddin Bâkır Çelebi: "Semâ is a servant's journey, where he would first reach the state of *fena (annihilation of the self, in complete union with Allah)* by orienting himself towards the Truth, relinquishing his *nafs*, and being exalted by love and wisdom; then he would return to servanthood, this time as a mature, perfect human."

What does the semâ ritual signify?

Semâ came to symbolize the Mevlevî Order, and the word became synonymous with the Order. Integrated with music and systemized by certain rules, the "whirling" act has, in time, become more majestic, impressive, and appealing to the soul. Pir Adil Chalabi (died 1490), one of Hz. Mevlânâ's great-grandchildren, more or less, finalized the form, as performed today, of "*semâ*". In time it was transformed into a ritual by Mevlevîs.

Each act in this ritual bears a meaning. From the particular shape of the ritual quarters called semâhane to the colours of the *post*, and from the dervish's garments to each of his movements, all is symbolic. For instance, the *semâhane* has a round floor to represent the world; the colour red of the *post* (sheepskin) on which the *sheikh* sits is regarded as Mevlânâ Celâleddîn-i Rûmî's abode, occupied by the *Sheikh Efendi* on his behalf. The colour red symbolizes "unity with Allah"; Hz. Mevlânâ united with his Allah at sunset. When the sun is rising and setting, the sky turns red. The red colour of the *sheikh post* similarly indicates departing life on Earth, the material realm, and rising into the spiritual life. The *post*, where beginners of Mevlevî Order sit, is black. In his "journey of enlightenment," the new initiate comes to earn a white "post."

As for the garments of a whirler, his *sikke* (traditional hat), shaped like a tombstone, symbolizes the tombstone of his *nafs* (ego), his *tennûre* (ritual gown), the shroud of his ego.

Today, a *semâ ritual* begins with *Nat-ı Sharif*, music in praise of our prophet Hz. Mohammad, as composed by Mustafa Itri Efendi (died 1712).

The sound of *kudüm* (drum) recalls Allah's command, "Be!" while creating the cosmos. This is followed by the sound of *ney* (reed flute), the divine breath! The Universe has been composed, and life has begun.

The whirlers *(semâzen)*[12], as led by *Sheikh Efendi*, follow a circular path around the *semâhâne* (whirling hall). Each semi-circle symbolizes the material world while the other half stands for the spiritual worlds. The completion of these three acts, called *Devr-i Veledi* (Cycle of of Sultan Veled), implies an initial orientation for a spiritual journey. As the *semâzen* begins the whirling ritual, he takes off his *hırka* (dervish coat) that symbolizes his *nafs*. This indicates *semâzen*'s stepping into purification. His arms crossed on his chest, represent the oneness of Allah. The *semâzen* begins revolving as he is granted permission by his sheikh; which is performed in the way that the *semâzen* kisses the hand of his sheikh, and the sheikh kisses the head of the *semâzen*.

---

12 Translator's Note: A Mevlevî dervish who whirls in a semâ ritual (Tur. *semâzen*) is commonly referred in the West as 'whirling dervish'. However, the term 'whirler' or its Turkish counterpart *semâzen* is preferred throughout the translated edition. It is observed that the term 'whirling dervish' is from time to time also ascribed to people who perform the act of whirling as a show (rather than a sacred ritual), often with commercial interests, and outside the act's authentic, traditional context.

Opening both arms to the sides and revolving from right to left, the *semâzen* emerges as embracing the entire universe. His right hand with the open palm extended up towards the sky indicates the act of receiving from *Haqq*. His left hand with the palm extended down towards the earth indicates distribution of grace among fellow men.

Semâ consists of four parts (four *selâms).* The first two *'selâm'*s signify elevation of the self by purification of the *nafs*, the third *selâm* signifies reaching a state of union with Allah, and the fourth *selâm* signifies the return of the self to servanthood, which is the ultimate purpose of man's creation. The *Sheikh Efendi* also joins the fourth *selâm,* symbolizing the absolute need for a spiritual guide while walking this path. The ritual ends with a Quran recitation and a prayer.

What about the significance of the semâ ritual for the semâzen and the audience?

As the *semâ* ritual concludes, both the dervish and the audience feel closer to the Almighty Creator. Their love for Allah strengthened, and their souls purified, they attain a contented and peaceful state of mind.

You are not in favor of the applause of the semâ ritual.

Yes, I am averse to it, because *semâ* is a *form* of *dhikr* (remembrance of Allah), it is a ritual, a religious ceremony. During *semâ*, a *semâzen* performs the act of whirling while uttering the holy *dhikr* Allah, applauding of which is deemed unseemly. During a ritual of that kind, an audience rather needs to focus on the private experience of the spirituality embodied by the ceremony. We witness that respect more often when we are abroad, for instance, our experiences in countries with Catholic populations: the ritual concludes with the Quran reading and finally the prayer, yet there's no sound to be heard in the hall. Oftentimes I stand up and offer a silent greeting, implying, "It is over..." but people begin to gaze with sadness when they understand it is finished. I say, "I would be happy to answer any questions you may have," but they don't ask much; instead, they remain silent in their seats, apparently to stay immersed in the spiritual atmosphere.

What is your view of those who do not show such respect?

Everybody is a *cân* (fellow soul), which we have to show respect. Each and every human being carries Allah's breath. Even the ones who come across as the most wicked do carry Allah's breath, which means goodness in essence. True wisdom lies in seeing and bringing out the good in people, not discarding them with labels like ill-behaved, wicked, etc.

Sometimes it proves to be a real challenge to forgive the ones who harm the path, but we must give them a second chance and tell them about the "good manners" of the way. As a mother, that's how I see it. I have a saying: "If you send your naughty child away, he will grow even naughtier." It may sound childish, but I think it is very important. We must, of course, prevent any wrongdoing that would harm the path.

We are happy to see you in almost all symposiums and panels on Hz. Mevlânâ. Even your presence alone brings a spiritual depth to these meetings. What is your source of motivation?

To the extent I could keep track of them, I absolutely prefer to participate in all symposiums and panels on Hz. Mevlânâ. Because I am aware of the effort it takes on the side of the speakers, that they read through volumes of books for a speech of mere twenty minutes. I respect these studies and am willing to serve the ones who serve the way of my ancestors; these have been the sources of my motivation. Also, the opportunity to benefit from the participants' knowledge. I think my presence pleases them, but it is me who feels the most content; I learn from these meetings.

I wish to serve the ones at the service of Hz. Pîr; this is a product of our upbringing, a perspective that we gained during childhood. I hope to find many more occasions to be of service; for instance, with "The Village Project" I try to create new opportunities for our esteemed professors. I hope that in the future, they will join us in the village and share their knowledge with the ones who will visit there to live and learn.

You've said you would like to provide support, to participate in the symposiums. What criteria should an event meet for that?

Provided that I hear about the event and it suits my schedule. That's it. Indeed, it is a priority for me. When I'm busy, I would rather work over the night at the expense of sleep than skipping those symposiums.

So, you would like to support all organizations without any differentiation.

Yes, that's true. I am trying to support and take part in all kinds of sincere efforts along the path of Hz. Pîr. Local and international events. When I had meniscus trouble, the doctor advised me not to walk, and I started to walk with a cane. In the airports, I reached the boarding gates using the special wheelchairs. Despite my condition, I went to Brazil, because there was an event about Hz. Pîr and I had been invited as a participant in a workshop. I went so that people can learn about Hz. Mevlânâ. I spent two days in São Paulo and joined some meetings as a speaker, on the third day we drove down the highway for two hours out of São Paulo and climbed a mountain for 45 minutes. What I saw was a group of bungalow houses in the heart of a wild forest, but more important than that, I was amazed by the semâhâne there.

The family who constructed this and invited me had a couple, a Brazilian lady and her Italian husband. Together, we performed salat in the semâhâne. That experience was above and beyond all. It was worth everything indeed. Praise to Allah, these are blessings of my Lord. Indeed, there is truth in the saying, "Do *khidmat* (service) to find *himmat* (grace and favor from the saints)." Praise to Allah, may my Lord render our services abound.

The family's culture of going beyond the call of duty in serving others started with Hz. Sultan Veled, is that correct?

The family is unparalleled in terms of service, support, and dissemination of these notions. I think the following couplet by Hz. Pîr serves as a key to understand his works:

"As long as I live, I am the slave of the Quran; I am the ground of chosen Mohammed's way.

Whoever carries a word of me apart from this, I am complainant of him, and I am complainant of those words too."[13]

So we try to be of service too, following the path that Hz. Pîr set for us. Neither our ancestors, nor our father, or we held back from serving others. Since we were born into this family, we must keep this culture alive, up-to-date, and pass it on to future generations. Our efforts will hopefully grow every single day and reach out to larger masses.

We are living in an era that resembles Hz. Pîr's time. Humanity all around the world is going through a difficult time. And this is the biggest reason why people put so much effort into reading Hz. Mevlânâ to understand his thought, why people seek wisdom in his words. In Hz. Pîr's time, the Mongolians posed a challenge. It is not clear to me we deal with whom today. Every single day new counterparts emerge, yet it is unclear where they come from and what they intend to do. May my Lord keep us safe from their harm and set them on the right path, may my Lord destine them to do good to others. People need to unite under the notion of seeing the good in things, and appreciating it; altogether, people need to join forces to convey beauty and goodness.

Togetherness and unity of the ones who serve...

Eyvallah (that is thankfully right), all the ones who are of service... We are no different from each other; we all serve the same cause. When I talk about that, sometimes I receive questions about the differences between religious orders (also known as *tariqahs/turuq*, or Sufi orders). While sharing the

13 Translator's Note: English translation by Feyzi Halıcı is taken from http://mevlana.net/mevlana.html.

same compass, you may still use different vehicles to reach a particular destination; you can take a plane, get on a ship, ride a bicycle, drive a car, or you can walk. Ways of traveling may vary, the resulting paths may look different from each other in length, etc., but in the end, they do reach the same destination. For that matter, I think the Sufi orders do not diverge in essence, but only in terms of their expressions. This should naturally be the case as all *tariqahs* share the same goal and refer to the same source: the Quran and the hadith (Prophet Mohammad's words); we are all guided by our Prophet Mohammad's way of life, we all serve my Lord and try to be worthy of our almighty creator in attempting to adopt the manners of our Prophet.

These meetings must have left you with some interesting memories. You are frequently traveling abroad on invitation, are there any anecdotes you would like to tell us from your visits to the far-away places like America, Brazil?

Thank Allah, my Lord blesses us with gifts every moment, as long as we notice and feel grateful. I can tell you about Dervish İsmail, who has a special place in my memories. I first met him in the United States when he came to hear one of my speeches. Afterward, he asked for my contact information, my email address. A few years later, I received an email from someone from the United States, saying he wanted to visit us in Konya. The date coincided with the time when Faruk Hemdem Çelebi and I planned to be in Konya. So we met.

After a while, he said he would like to visit again. This time, however, was quite different. He sounded more informed.

During our conversations, he told us that he was a Catholic priest, who was raised accordingly, yet he was still on a search while our paths crossed; after listening to my speech in the United States, he made further research before visiting me and decided to go deeper before his second visit. He was teaching "Monotheist Religions" at university in the United States.

Anyways, during a few days, Faruk Hemdem Çelebi, myself and *Sheikh Master* Nâdir Karnıbüyükler altogether spent time with him; we talked and tried to answer his questions. One late-afternoon, Faruk Çelebi suggested, "The tomb is about to be closed. Let's go and visit; I feel like it."

I didn't join them, as I'd been there about an hour ago. So the three of them, named Faruk Çelebi, Nâdir *Dede,* and the gentleman whose name I could never memorize, visited the tomb. There, Nâdir *Dede* prayed and recited verses from the Quran. When the gentleman came back to the hotel, he had a very different expression on his face. I wanted to tell him something, but again, couldn't remember his name although we were together for the last few days, I'd seen him several times. So I turned to him and said, "Please accept my apologies for failing to remember your name. May I call you İsmail? You have a smiling face, 'smile' would help me memorize İsmail." His eyes were suddenly filled with tears as he replied: "I would be very glad."

Later, he told me that he experienced a peculiar state while hearing the Quran recitation in the tomb and that he thought his name was sent by Allah the moment I called him "İsmail" after he returned from the tomb. And he asked of Nâdir Dede, "I want to take some lessons, I want to learn more." It must be during the 4-5 years that followed, that he spent all his summer holidays in Konya, where he stayed at least 1-2 months, and spent his money earned from teaching on learning thoroughly about Islam, which he took as his duty. He recorded the Quran recitations of Nâdir Dede and kept wearing earphones all the time, by listening to which, he memorized the verses. Later, he recited the *Kalimah Shahadat* and became a Muslim. And during a symposium, when it was his turn to speak, we heard how he presented himself. He held up his name card, which revealed his name in English. In his very good Turkish, he said: "I only carry this name in my passport." Then he turned the back of the card and greeted the audience with his hand over heart: "I'm dervish İsmail."

Photograph 46: Dervish İsmail in semâ, at the Vatican.

Back then, İsmail was above fifty, not a child but a conscious adult. Meanwhile, he wanted to understand Islam in its Arabic context, and to learn the prayers in Arabic. He also started to learn Persian to have a deeper understanding of Hz. Mevlânâ. He married a young Azerbaijani lady whom he met in Konya. They are now living in the United States, traveling back and forth between here and there as needed. He gave us this beautiful experience, may Allah bless him with peace, may his path be clear.

We have many such stories. I mean, we have a lot of companions abroad who know of Islam and Hz. Mevlânâ at the level of teaching (as a *sheikh*). In the United States, Holland, Germany, and Iran, they have established foundations under the local legislation of their countries. They are liaised with us, getting our moral support. We share knowledge, they ask for our guidance on what and how to do. Some of these Sheikh Masters were authorized and appointed by my father Celâleddin Bâkır Çelebi, and many others by my dear Faruk Hemdem Çelebi, my brother, my spiritual elder.[14]

There is another story, again, about a foreign fellow. Maybe we can write this one without disclosing his name. It was during the time of flower people that he came with his backpack. A good-looking, nice young man. He planned to travel to the East, a hitchhiking journey. On his way, he was picked up by a truck. When they reached a turn in the dark of the night, he got off and walked for a while. He then slipped into his sleeping bag and slept the night under a tree. In the morning, he woke up to a beautiful voice reciting *azan* (call to salat, prayer performed by Muslims five times a day), which enchanted him as he listened. He got up and noticed something moving, an elderly person doing things that involve bowing and standing. Once finished, the man approached him. It turned out that he was a local from a nearby village. The young man, who

14 See: Bayru, Esin Çelebi and Şimşekler, Nuri, *Mevlâna'dan Mevlâ'ya Ulaşanlar: Yurt Dışındaki Yabancı Mevlevîler*, International Mevlâna Foundation, Konya, 2012.

had difficulty finding his way beyond the tree in the dark, was unaware of that village. With the local villager's invitation for him to stay there as a guest, it seemed as if the whole experience (watching the salat, listening to *azan*) invited him to a new direction. Afterward, he researched Islam. He was on a search anyways. After all, it was what had set him on a journey that brought him all the way up here. Today, he is a Muslim who tells about Islam to people around him.

I see a bustling crowd around us. Those who visit from within the town, out of town, and abroad. It's like a gathering point of people from all walks of life. You must be experiencing interesting encounters among these. For example, this morning, Güzîde Hanımefendi mentioned about the Japanese doctor, who came here to explore the impact of semâ on humans. Can you tell us a bit about that?

Well, interestingly enough, it was his first time here. He is a medical doctor and a practitioner of acupuncture. He travels to the energy spots on earth and explores his topic by directly feeling the energy in these places. It's what brought him to Konya. He walked into the shrine with earphones that generate sounds which describe everything about the surroundings. When he stood in the presence of Hz. Pîr -I mean in front of his sarcophagus- the sound suddenly disappeared into complete silence. First, he thought the machine broke. But he heard sounds again when he moved a little further, and silence when he's back to the spot. Then he took off the earphones and stood there, to feel the energy. Just waited there with eyes closed, hands open. I asked him: "A beautiful energy surrounded you, am I right? A very soft one." He said: "Yes, indeed. I felt that kind of vibe all around myself, which was a quite moving experience. I mostly encountered harsh energies in the places I visited before. For the first time, I felt enveloped by such mellow, all-embracing energy. This had a great impact on me."

He came to visit us in the foundation after seeing the shrine. His interpreter was a lady who spoke Turkish very fluently. I told them about the *semâ* ritual, describing it along with the deeper symbolic meanings of the rituals. Then I invited them to one, where he sat next to me and watched the *Âyin-i Sharif* with the relevant knowledge which fascinated him. Later, he asked if he could meet the whirlers, and did so, while staying in Konya over the next few days.

In the end, he decided: he was going to visit Konya every year to treat the whirlers with acupuncture, helping the ones with aches, accepting whoever wished to have a treatment. He later wrote in a letter: "I would like to treat you and ten people from your friends. It will be at no cost. So long as I can be of service." So he came over and served like that, perhaps for five-six years. We are thankful to him. He helped many.

Among celebrities and politicians from Turkey or across the world, there are followers of Hz. Mevlânâ, quoting his messages in their words, who became Mevlevî, who are in touch with you. Is that correct?

It wouldn't be right to cite names, but there are many world-wide known figures who admire Hz. Mevlânâ, who read his works. They write novels, screenplays, they paint and sculpt. The politicians quote Hz. Mevlânâ's words in their speech-es. Madonna and Crist, who leads the famous Coltlui, are important names who deliver messages about Hz. Mevlânâ.

They mentioned about their intention to visit. Do you have any information?

Many years ago, Madonna wanted to produce a clip where she would appear in a *semâzen* costume. While my father was in the United States, her agent reached him and asked for permission. When my father explained the symbolic meaning of the *semâzen* costume, they apologized, and Madonna decided not to wear it. She had shown decency. We also know that she composed songs based on Hz. Mevlânâ's words. I think she feels a genuine affinity and respect. As I said, we get to know many kinds of people: there are those who watched a semâ ritual, who heard a poem of Hz. Mevlânâ, or a sound of reed flute, there are those who visited here after they saw him in their dreams. These first encounters excite me. People read and search. I'd like to say, how lucky they are. We had many such guests from a variety of regions like southern Africa, Tanzania, America, Europe, also from Pakistan, India, Japan, and Korea. These people are moved by what I will call as a love of Hz. Pîr. They search for the meaning of Hz. Mevlânâ's words that touched them. They come all the way to Konya, seeking more information. We have conversations with broadcasters, journalists, and writers who visit here. They do interviews and publish these in their countries. I met people who came to Konya to meet me, who said: "I've seen you before, on TV."

Eva de Vitray Meyerovitch had an interesting story too, correct? Her remains had been transferred to Konya after ten years.

Eva de Vitray Meyerovitch later adopted the name Havva, had a beautiful life story. Initially raised as a Catholic, her path crossed at some point with Hz. Pîr and she began to study his thought, eventually becoming a Muslim. She was a university professor in France. She also established an institute in her country. In a conference, she stated a wish: "Bury me in the shadow of Hz. Mevlânâ." My father knew her; she had also visited our house. She used to visit Konya and was invited to the symposiums in Istanbul.

She had two sons, whom her students approached and spoke about her will when she died in France. But they couldn't accept, unwilling to let their mother rest in a place so far from them. After the burial in France, her students persisted. It turned out the French legislation didn't allow the transfer of mortal remains after 10th anniversary of burial. As the date approached, her students in France and Turkey gathered, and kindly informed the children: "Now is the last time for rendering your mother's wish, will you please permit us?" This time, apparently, with an eased sense of grief, they allowed. In any case, it wasn't an easy task. There were bureaucratic procedures involving the requirements of both governments. With serious efforts, the remains of (Eva) Havva *Hanım* reached Turkey on December 17, 2008, on a *Şeb-i Arûs* anniversary. Ten years after her decease, upon the funeral prayer, she was buried in the Üçler Cemetery. There was a huge crowd, including ministers, MPs, the governor, the mayor, and people from many different countries, standing altogether by the grave. I was there too.

It was during the burial when *Hodja*s began to recite prayers, I saw *Hâfız* İsmail *Bey,* a visually impaired *Hodja*. He was asking to partake in the prayer, but they brushed him aside, although he had a better voice than them and was quite knowledgeable. The person who accompanied him couldn't help either. Watching from a distance, I felt upset. So I turned to the journalist gentleman standing next to me: "Could you please ask him if he could stay here when the ceremony is over? After everyone leaves, let us recite a prayer together." And he passed on my message. It is interesting... What I noticed in *Hâfız* İsmail *Bey,* I'd seen before in Kâni *Hodja*: they looked around reflexively as if they were able to see.

People left after the recitation. There was no one but us and a guided group of tourists from various countries, who frequently visited the place out of their loyalty to Hz. Pîr. I approached them and asked, "Please come and join us; let us say a prayer together." They said, "Dear Çelebi, all the prayers were said already." I suggested, "Never mind, there's no such thing as surplus when it comes to reading the Qur'an; let's repeat the prayers." An *aşir* (prayer after salat) was recited again; then I recited a *gülbang* (prayer blessing holy people from the Mevlevî lineage). Then, a professor from India who spent his life mostly in the United States said other prayers. And a Spanish lady asked for permission to chant a hymn in her language. A French lady followed her. In the end, the group said prayers, chanted hymns in different languages like Arabic, Turkish, English, Spanish, French. We finished by reciting the dhikr of Allah and a final prayer. It was a great gift, a real blessing from Allah. We humans, we must realize and appreciate these when we are alive. Allah's blessings are boundless. The story of Eva Hanım is something that I tell to the young people as an example. My Lord is such that a servant can be blessed with gifts even ten years after walking to *Haqq*, after burial. This is a really pleasant memory.

I guess it was three or four years later; a group came to visit from the United States. Mostly university professors, lecturers, and instructors. A lady among them asked about the place of Eva Hanım's grave. I said the tomb was quite close to the foundation, and also told her this story. Her eyes filled with tears, she said, "I'm a student of hers. After she passed away, I conducted research on her life story, recollected her memories, and wrote her biography. But, somehow, I couldn't manage to publish the book. It's been years. Now I understand... I was actually waiting for this story. Please let me add this to the end of the biography." I said, "There's even a photograph; I should give it to you then." When I handed it to her, she said: "Now, the book is complete." Later, I heard that the biography went to press.

Photograph 47: At the grave of Eva de Vitray Meyerovitch.

As we know, you received an honorary Ph.D. from the United States.

Yes. It is from a university in Berkeley, named Starr King School for the Ministry, which is actually a faculty of theology.

I had met one of their professors during his travels. İbrahim Farajajé, an Indian-American professor who taught courses on Islam at the university. May Allah bless his soul, we lost him last year. He followed my studies for some time, and then submitted a proposal to the university committee to nominate myself for the award of an honorary Ph.D. The professors conducted assessment for a year, and the award was approved unanimously on the next annual council meeting after the proposal. It came as a surprise; I wasn't informed before. I received a letter, well written in Turkish, which informed me about their intention to award an honorary Ph.D. in recognition of my contributions in the topic of world peace, and it said they would like to invite me if I accept. The award ceremony was going to take place as part of the graduation ceremony at the end of the semester. I was thrilled about the news. The ceremony was beautiful. I was joined by my friends from the United States and even a spiritual daughter of mine, Dr. Ayşegül from Turkey. It was a great event.

We were transported via car from Berkeley to the venue, which was the largest church in San Francisco -I had no idea where we were going. Everything was exquisitely planned, such that in the indoor parking space of the church, I noticed my name on a tag to reserve the closest parking slot to the elevator. I was directed to a room, where we, the participants, were asked to wear their ceremony robes. I was there with the students. Then a lady lined us up; I was going to walk as the last one in the row.

There was another recipient of honorary Ph.D., a 93-year-old lady who was waiting in a reserved seat in the ceremony hall. She was the wife of the school's founder and had served the school for many years.

We entered the hall, walking through a corridor of all the professors working there, amid their applause. In the background, there was organ music and voices chanting hymns -I don't know much about these, but it must certainly be of significance to them.

My seat was the first one in the second row, next to my friends. The students also sat in the front rows, and the professors took their positions on the stage. After the President delivered the commencement address, they lit a candle as a ritual to initiate the ceremony. İbrahim Efendi's son İsa recited *azan* in the church, with a voice trained by the *muezzin* of the Süleymaniye Mosque. For me, that was a greater gift than the honorary title itself. Then a professor spoke about me and invited me to the stage. It was exhilarating. The President presented me the certificate denoting the honorary title, in a framed pane.

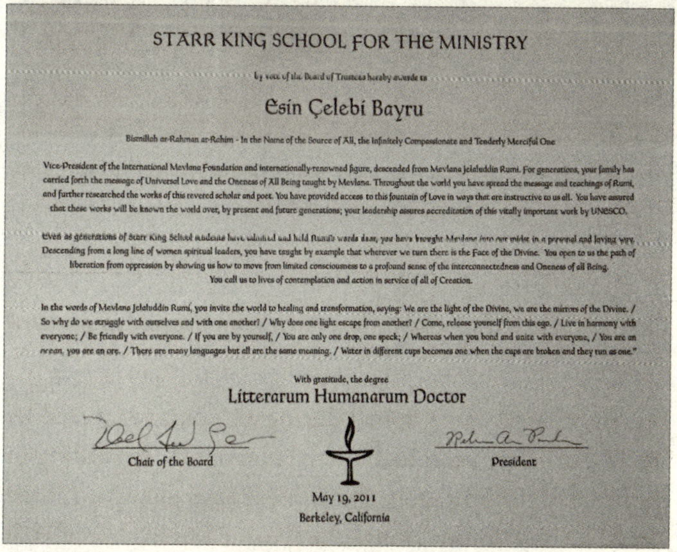

STARR KING SCHOOL FOR THE MINISTRY

by vote of the Board of Trustees hereby awards to

Esin Çelebi Bayru

Bismillah ar-Rahman ar-Rahim - In the Name of the Source of All, the Infinitely Compassionate and Tenderly Merciful One

Vice-President of the International Mevlana Foundation and internationally-renowned figure, descended from Mevlana Jelaluddin Rumi. For generations, your family has carried forth the message of Universal Love and the Oneness of All Being taught by Mevlana. Throughout the world you have spread the message and teachings of Rumi, and further researched the works of this revered scholar and poet. You have provided access to this fountain of Love in ways that are instructive to us all. You have assured that these works will be known the world over, by present and future generations; your leadership assures accreditation of this vitally important work by UNESCO.

Even as generations of Starr King School students have studied and held Rumi's words dear, you have brought Mevlana into our midst in a personal and loving way. Descending from a long line of women spiritual leaders, you have taught by example that wherever we turn there is the Face of the Divine. You open to us the path of liberation from oppression by showing us how to move from limited consciousness to a profound sense of the interconnectedness and Oneness of all Being. You call us to lives of contemplation and action in service of all of Creation.

In the words of Mevlana Jelaluddin Rumi, you invite the world to healing and transformation, saying: We are the light of the Divine, we are the mirrors of the Divine. / So why do we struggle with ourselves and with one another? / Why does one light escape from another? / Come, release yourself from this ego. / Live in harmony with everyone; / Be friendly with everyone. / If you are by yourself, / You are only one drop, one speck; / Whereas when you bond and unite with everyone, / You are an ocean, you are an ore. / There are many languages but all are the same meaning. / Water in different cups becomes one when the cups are broken and they run as one."

With gratitude, the degree

Litterarum Humanarum Doctor

Chair of the Board

President

May 19, 2011

Berkeley, California

Photograph 48: The Certificate of Honorary Doctorate.

Prof. İbrahim Farajajé put the white graduation collar around my neck. As they asked me to deliver a speech, I read Hz. Mevlânâ's advice to his son which I had collected earlier. And İbrahim Efendi read the English version of it. I thanked them and took my seat. It was about three or four years after the ceremony; they visited Konya. While handing my cap and gown to me, they said: "You are now a council member at our university."

Photograph 49: İbrahim Farajá ve Rebecca Parker, at the Honorary Doctorate Ceremony of Esin Çelebi Bayru.

Can you also tell us about the charter of citizenship granted in Khoy?

Yes, the charter was granted during an event organized by the MP of Khoy, who had invited me to join. According to the belief of the Iranian people, once Hazrat Shams-i Tabrizi served his mission in Konya, he returned to his homeland, Tabrizi region, and began to teach at a madrasa in the city of Khoy. I don't know whether this takes reference from a reliable source or not. But that's how it is described in the oral history.

I visited the city on an invitation to the event I mentioned. Before the trip, I shared the news with my friends too. An Iranian lady said: "We are originally from Khoy, my family migrated to Turkey in my grandfather's time. My great-uncle had a photo of the madrasa and mosque. My grandfather was very interested in these; he had invited a specialist photographer from Europe, and had many places in Iran photographed. We had these. But my uncle donated the picture to the Sabancı Museum. As far as I could remember, the mosque in the photograph had three minarets; it was part of a large social complex including a mosque and a madrasa." When I visited the place, I noticed that only one of the minarets was left standing, and the area around was cleaned up. The minaret's walls were paved with tiles and animal horns.

It signified the following: whenever people constructed a mosque in the name of a holy personage, they sacrificed animals during the construction to pay tribute to that person and distributed the meat to the workers there. While the meat became a meal, the horns were placed in the wall. They have this tradition. So, people there claim that the horns in the wall belonged to the animals sacrificed in honor of Hazrat Shams, and the grave there is his tomb. It is what they believe. I don't know whether it is true or not.

In my address there, I spoke along the following lines: "I don't know where the soil-body of Hz. Shams actually returned back to the soil, which is where it birthed from. Even in Konya, people mention three different places. I mean, even there is a shrine, which is thought to be of Hz. Shams in Konya, there are still other spots mentioned. There's also mention of a place in Pakistan, in the north of India. I think we must leave it to the researchers. What really matters to us is what we can learn from the thought of Hz. Shams. And how can we transform our lives with these learnings?" If I had taken a stance, it wouldn't mean much. I can't give a certain answer about something I don't know. There, I received the "Charter of Fellow Citizenship," an ornate work of Persian calligraphy. It, of course, made me very happy. Thank Allah.

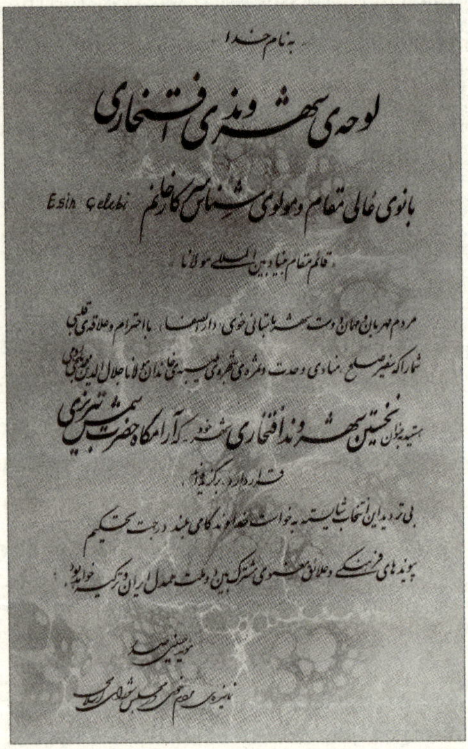
به نام خدا

لوحه‌ی شهروندی افتخاری

بانوی عالی مقام و مولوی شناس کارعلم Esin Çelebi

قائم مقام بنیاد بین المللی مولانا

مردم مهربان و مهمان دوست شهر باستانی خوی (دارالصفا) با احترام و علاقه‌ی قلبی

شما را که سفیر صلح، منادی وحدت و مژده‌ی شهروندی [illegible] خاندان مولانا جلال الدین محمد بلخی

هستید به عنوان نخستین شهروند افتخاری شهر خود که آرامگاه حضرت شمس تبریزی

قرار دارد، برگزیده‌ام.

بی تردید این انتخاب شایسته به خواست خداوند گامی بلند در جهت تحکیم

پیوندهای فرهنگی و علایق معنوی مشترک بین دو ملت همدل ایران و ترکیه خواهد بود.

محمد حسین

نماینده‌ی مردم خوی در مجلس شورای اسلامی

Photograph 50: Charter of Fellow Citizenship, City of Khoy, Tabrizi Region of Iran.

Hazrat Mevlânâ attracts attention around the world. At least this is the case for the intelligentsia. What could be the reasons for this universal appeal?

To tell the truth, people abroad are more knowledgeable. There are people who were moved by a poem, music, a dream that made them curious, or by watching a semâ ritual; they researched what they saw, and obtained knowledge. Many of them even carried this to the level of choosing the path of Islam through the Mevlevî Way. What lies underneath Hz. Mevlânâ's broad appeal is the way he fuses the love of *Haqq* (a holy name of Allah) with the love of humanity. He embarked on an inner journey of self-discovery and realized that whatever he saw deep inside him was all that he shared in common with others.

Hz. Pîr says: "O come, come and let us appreciate each other. Because you never know, we may suddenly fall apart. If our Prophet said, 'One Muslim is a mirror to another,' why would we turn away from the mirror? Hatred and grudges would cast a shadow on the friendship and wound the heart. Then why don't we root out the grudges from our hearts?"

Could we say that Mathnawi, a cultural treasure that we have, draws more interest from the West than here because our people are unaware of what they possess -or perhaps uncaring?

In fact, both. We are acting like spenders. As we chase after ready-made, we find it rather difficult to seek knowledge through our own efforts, we shy away from reading, researching, studying. On the other hand, we need to protect the values of Hz. Mevlânâ and the Mevlevî Way, which forms an important part of our cultural heritage. For that, we must study and digest it well. Those who are in search of the truth, I would like to remind them of the following advice of Hz. Mevlânâ:

There is a life in you, search for that life,
Search for the secret jewel in the mountain of your body,
Hey you, the passing away friend, look with all your strength,
Whatever you are looking for, look in yourself not around.[15]

When Hazrat Mevlânâ walked to Haqq, people of all creeds came to his funeral. There, Christians, Jews, and people from other religions wept together with Muslims.

People saw their own nature, their faith in Hz. Mevlânâ. What defined him above all else was that he never looked down on others; he acted forgivingly and saw the good in them.

Let me mention how Eflakî describes the funeral of Hz. Mevlânâ: People of all nations and religions were there. From Turks to Arabs, from Christians to Jews. They walked with the books of their faith, recited sacred lines from the Psalms, the Torah, the Gospel. They wailed. The Muslims attempted to drive them away. They refused. As the stand-off escalated into a great tumult, people informed the Sultan and his men. So they summoned and questioned the rabbis, priests, and bishops there: "This is a funeral of our revered religious leader, our saint. What has it got to do with you?" And they replied: "We learned from his lucid words the truth about our prophets and their messages, we saw in him the good manners

15 Translator's Note: English translation is taken from: http://mevlana.net/works.html.

of the saints and prophets that were described in our holy books. Just as you Muslims revere him as the Muhammed of his age, we deem him to be the Moses, the Jesus of our time. We are attached to him a thousand times deeper than you; we are his friends." Hz. Pîr had said: "The seventy-two nations hear their secrets from us. We are the reed-flute that sings hundreds of notes in one fret."

It's been also said: "Hz. Mevlânâ is the sun of truth that shines above humanity. Everyone loves the sun. All houses are lit with its rays."

And a Roman priest declared: "Mevlânâ is like bread. Everyone needs bread. Have you ever seen a hungry man running away from it?"

With that, everyone went silent. People saw their own nature, their faith in Hz. Mevlânâ. What defined him above all else was that he never looked down on others; he acted forgivingly and saw the good in people.

We observe that Hazrat Mevlânâ and the Mevlevî Culture gained popularity, particularly after the 90's. What could be the possible reasons behind that?

The human soul is hungry... I think the reason why Hz. Mevlânâ attracted a growing amount of research interest and curiosity in recent years is this: over the last century, under the influence of the Western culture, people came to value materiality above all else. Who can make more money? How to climb one's way up by stepping on the shoulders of others? That was the teaching of the last century. People strived in their race to attain top-notch wealth. The best cars, the greatest houses. Yet, when they reached the climax of the best facades, they began to notice their emptiness inside...

What we call human is the togetherness of body and soul, the interplay of form and essence. Only spiritual things can satisfy a hungry soul. Over the years, people grew unhappy as they stuffed their material facade and starved their souls. I've noticed that people from all parts of the world share the following in common: when in search of meaning, they first study their own religion, then explore the other ones. They look into Buddhism or Hinduism, yet draw only limited insights due to distortions that misrepresent such belief systems as just some kind of gymnastic, and people miss the essence of it.

But, at one point during their search, they encounter Hz. Pîr and his description of the path of divine love within the context of Islam, which leads them to study Hz. Mevlânâ's thought and works.

I think the best part of all is that they come to learn about Islam. There are many people around us today, who have adopted Islam through Hz Pîr's Way. On that, we have a book named: "Those Who Reach from Mevlânâ to Mawla," prepared by my dear professor Nuri Şimşekler and myself. This book alone would, of course, fall short of providing a full account. We need larger volumes.

The stories of the many beautiful people we've encountered is a whole other thing. What upsets us the most is the misrepresentation of the Mevlevî Order as a non-religious, un-Islamic phenomenon. Quite the contrary, the Quran and hadiths had been the primary sources that inspired Hz. Mevlânâ. The veteran experts call his Masnavî "a *tafsir* (interpretation of the Qur'an)." We must keep these in mind. And yes: striking a balance between our material and spiritual lives is the key to find lasting peace, a quest that led many people to find Hz. Pîr.

On your remark, "the influence of the Western culture"... Besides the waves of materialism, there are also waves of philosophy: ideas that we can't possibly put into practice. In contrast, Hazrat Mevlânâ presents a unique style with the practical notions prescribed in the Masnavî.

First of all, Hz. Mevlânâ is not a philosopher, although that's how some people refer to him in the West. For us the Turkish nation, Hz. Mevlânâ is a *friend of Allah (wali)*, an heir to the Prophet Muhammad, therefore a master of spirituality. We must keep this in mind. The term *wali* doesn't have a direct equivalent in the Western languages. Instead, they have the one-word concept of the saint, like in "Saint Paul," which is not the same.

When Hz. Pîr is called a "philosopher"; I feel saddened and step in to correct. Because Hz. Mevlânâ's thought actually describes a life-style based on Islam.

As we know, he didn't establish a religious order himself. He did not position himself as a leader of a religious movement; he rather was a *wali* who befriended Allah through his deep love and affinity for the Prophet Muhammad. These are also evident in his family story. A reason why the family left Balkh was the conflict between the philosophers and the Sufis of the time. Of course, the primary reason was the imminent danger of Mongol invasion.

There are those who claim to be a Mevlevî elder (Dede). They make comments like: "I am the successor of Mevlânâ, I am the grandmaster of the order, the holder of the red sheepskin. A lot of people concurrently saw this in their dream. The descendants of Hazrat Mevlânâ recognized me as their sheikh master." What is your take on this?

Throughout its history, the Mevlevî Order has been headed by the descendants of Hz. Mevlânâ. Those who wish to learn about this can refer to the books describing the customs of the Mevlevî tradition. After our father walked to *Haqq*, we made a joint decision as his children. Our upbringing was centered on love and peace, not on discord. We feel that it is our duty to serve Hz. Pir's way in the best manner, while it is not our business to react to such comments, which we have steered clear from. Our efforts speak for themselves. The works of our foundation were assessed and accredited by UNESCO, which is recognized as the most prominent institution in world culture. The International Mevlana Foundation is the sole institution that gained such official recognition on the topic of the Mevlevî Culture and Tradition.

Are there other people in Turkey who are known as "Çelebi"s? Do you know them? Are they also offering good services for the Mevlevî Order?

First, let me mention some special terms of the Mevlevî tradition—descendants of Hazrat Mevlânâ from the side of their father and mother are called differently, as *Zükur Çelebi* and *İnas Çelebi* respectively. Both male and female descendants assume the same title. We are among the Zükur Çelebis. There are many other descendants of Hz. Mevlânâ.

Our doors are open to all of them so that we can join forces and serve under the roof of the Foundation. We are here for whoever wants to join the efforts and be of service. If we carry the same blood, then we are one.

The posts of Dede (Mevlevî elder) and Chief Master (Maqam Chalabi). Why have these been only assumed by men? Are there any female Chief Masters? You are making efforts to promote Hazrat Mevlânâ to the world, what is your perspective on that?

We are talking about a history of more or less 800 years. Chief Masters have been elected from among the lineage of Hz. Mevlânâ's son, Sultan Veled. Sultan Veled and his son Ulu Arif Chalabi put Hz. Mevlânâ's teachings in a systematic framework, and established the first Mevlevî house, like a school, in the building adjoining Hz. Mevlânâ's tomb. We can think of the Mevlevî houses like boarding schools that only accepted male candidates who were past the age of puberty. In those times, the girls were not sent to school at all - I'm not referring to a Turkish or Muslim tradition; that was the practice in the whole world.

Although girls took the backseat in terms of receiving the formal education within the context of a centuries-old tradition, they were not denied learning; their information requests were always met. And if you'll notice, *semâhanes* (*whirling halls*) have a section specially reserved for ladies. Here, they watched and sometimes performed *semâ* rituals, and listened to discourses on Masnavî. Today there are a lot of women who do meaningful services for our path. They are from a variety of nations: Turkish, German, Italian, French,

American, and so on. Some have even studied Hz. Mevlânâ directly in Persian and translated his words to their native languages. I partly lived in their time. While they studied Hz. Pir's works, they felt that at one point, the translations fell short of conveying the whole meaning and decided to learn Persian to deepen their understanding. Later, they worked on the translation of Hz. Mevlânâ's works and took their knowledge to the level of adopting Islam.

I live for service, which I try to do with the permission of my brother and my spiritual elder, Faruk Hemdem Çelebi. We are five siblings. Five of us, with the ones close to our family, and followers of our path- altogether, we serve under the roof of the International Mevlana Foundation. The reason why I'm here for this interview is my family's decision to appoint me as their spokesperson. There are also occasions when we, me and my brother Faruk Hemdem Çelebi, are invited in TV broadcasts.

Besides us, our children also began to be of service, which is most gratifying. Thank Allah.

Throughout his time, Mevlânâ held women in high esteem.

First of all, let's remind ourselves of the perspective of Hazrat Muhammad, who respected women throughout his life. When his companions (*sahâbe)* asked who deserves the highest respect, he responded: "Your mothers!" Only after the same question was repeated and he gave the same answer three times, he replied: "Your fathers!" in the fourth time to make a point on the value of women. Our Prophet reserved special times to inform women with his discourses, responding to their questions. At the end of the Bedir War, the slaves were freed on the condition that they taught reading to ten male or female companions (*sahâbe*). This supports the view that knowledge must be equally available to women and men.

In essence, Islam does not discriminate men and women in terms of their value but takes into consideration the physiological and psychological differences between them. In the end, Islam submits women and men to each other, to complete each other and form a unified whole.

"As long as I live, I am the slave of the Quran.
I am the ground of chosen Mohammed's way.
Whoever carries a word of me apart from this,
I am complainant of him, and I am complainant of those words too."[16]

These words express Hazrat Mevlânâ Celâleddîn-i Rûmî's loyalty, his boundless affinity, and submission to Hazrat Muhammad. Could he ever speak or behave against the Quran?

In any case, Hz. Mevlânâ was against the idea of an oppressive culture that left women uneducated, one that confined them in their houses and hid them under the clothes far beyond the necessities of decorum. These are not just the thoughts he voiced. He formed a living example.

Hz. Mevlânâ pursued a monogamous life. He married Kerra *Hatun* after the death of his first wife Gevher Hatun, whom he had married at a young age. And he rejected the notion of people being slave and servant to anything and anyone, other than Allah.

16 Translator's Note: English translation by Feyzi Halıcı is taken from http://mevlana.net/mevlana.html.

The following advice from his letter to his son Sultan Veled reveals Hz. Mevlânâ's perspective on marriage: "For Allah's sake, if you want to honor yourself, your father, your ancestors: hold your wife very, very dear. If you want to steal her heart and appeal to her soul, live each day like it's your first and every night like your wedding night."

Let me quote Hz. Mevlânâ's words from the first volume of the Masnavî, which convey his view that marriage calls for equality and compatibility:

"We're a married couple; mates must be alike
In order that their affairs may turn out right
Each mate must be the other's similitude
Consider a pair of shoes or a pair of boots
If one of the shoes is too tight for the foot
You'll have no use for either of the two shoes
Have you seen one small and one large double door?
Or a lion mate with a wolf in the forest?
Loads don't balance on the back of a camel
If one's of short weight and the other is full"[17]

Hz. Mevlânâ treated his daughter, wives, and daughters-in-law kindly, with love and compassion. He gave lessons to women, visited them, conversed with them, attended gatherings organized by them, and performed semâ with them. Sultan Rükneddin's wife Gömeç *Hatun*, Muineddin-i Pervane's wife Gürcü *Hatun* were among the women who organized meetings at their houses. While they moved from Konya to Kayseri, Gürcü Hatun's family wished to have a painter named Aynüddevle make a portrait of Hz. Mevlânâ.

17 Translator's Note: English translation taken from: "Kenan Rıfâî, *Listen (Commentary on the Spiritual Couplets of Mevlana Rumi)*, Trans.: Victoria Rowe Holbrook, Fons Vitae Publishing, İstanbul, 2011".

Yet, the painter failed in all his attempts as the expression on Hz. Mevlânâ's face that mirrored his inner world kept changing.

In all his works, Hz. Mevlânâ talks about women and certain states of their nature. For example, we observe that in *Fîhi Mâ Fîh*, he says:

"What is woman, what is the world? Whether you say something or not, whatever is, is. It will not desist from what it does. It gets even worse as you give warning of it. If it is in nature of woman not to do evil, whether you say do or don't, she will follow her good nature, clean essence, and behave accordingly. If, on the contrary, her nature is corrupt, she will follow her own path. In truth to say, please don't do this or that, don't expose yourself, increases desires, and serves no other purpose."[18]

Then he presents a different angle: *"Woman is the light of God, not just the beloved. It is as if she is creative, not created"*[19], an aphorism reflecting the value he attached to women.

There are many examples denoting the importance of women in the early ages of the Mevlevî tradition. In Konya, Sultan Veled's daughter Şeref *Hatun* enlightened the people around her. She had many disciples, both men and women. In Tokat, there was Arife-i Hoşlika. In Afyon Karahisar, Destine Hatun (a grandchild of Divane Mehmet *Chalabi*) had a voice in the Mevlevî House. She wore *sikke* (traditional Mevlevî hat) and *hırka* (dervish coat). Later, again in Karahisar, we see Güneş Han (the daughter of little Mehmet *Chalabi*), who

18 Translator's Note: English translation is taken from http://mevlana.net/views_on_women.html.

19 Translator's Note: English translation is taken from http://mevlana.net/views_on_women.html.

held the position of Mevlevî *caliph* and *sheikh*. Likewise, Güneş Han-ı Suğra (the daughter of little Arif *Chalabi*) is among the women who assumed the role of *sheikh*.

And today, I can mention many names who have been following this path, sharing their knowledge with us, such as Anna Masala, Camille Helminski, Rabia Christine Brodbeck, Sachiko Murata, voiced Mevlânâ's words in German, English, Italian, French, and Chinese. Sâmiha Ayverdi, Nezihe Araz, Sofi Huri, Meliha Ambarcıoğlu, Gönül Ayan, Emine Yeniterzi, Barihüda Tanrıkorur, Hülya Küçük, Meşkûre Sargut, Cemâlnur Sargut, and Nur Hayat Artıran. It's been my honor to know them.

When talking about the Islamic and Mevlevî perspective on women, I must also mention how highly the Turks, especially Atatürk, valued women. Even in times when Turks lived in nomadic tents in Central Asia, the rulers invited women to meetings to take their views before making important decisions. Later in Ottoman times, the mothers of the sultans appeared as highly involved in a number of state affairs.

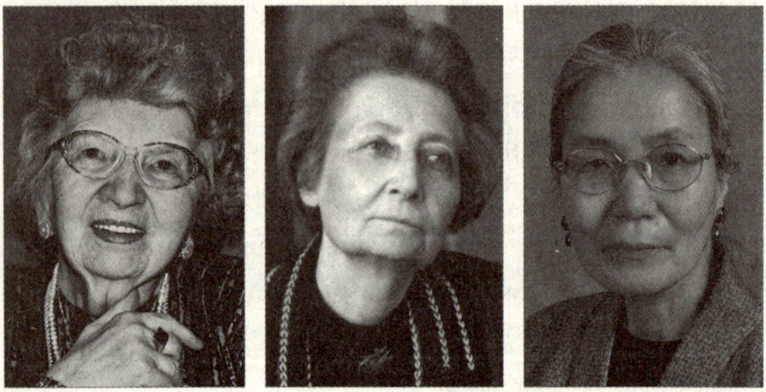

Photograph 51: Annamarie Schimmel, Sâmiha Ayverdi, Sachiko Murata.

Photograph 52: Sofi Huri, Camille Helminski, Anna Masala.

Photograph 53: Emine Yeniterzi, Nur Hayat Artıran, Cemâlnur Sargut.

On October 26, 1933, The Turkish Grand National Assembly chaired by Mustafa Kemal Atatürk, founder of the Republic of Turkey, enacted a law - a first in World history - that granted women the right to elect and be elected. Since these times, we see women in the parliament. Even if their number is few, Turkish women have a voice in the politics of Turkey.

If the mothers who give birth to future generations, who educate them first, and the teachers who are mostly women could realize how much power and influence they have, they can change the world. If they grow cognizant of the need to educate children as much on spirituality as material topics, the world would be a better, peaceful place.

Do people understand your ancestor Hazrat Mevlânâ's messages well? What is your perspective, in all positive and negative aspects, on the present-day perception of Hz. Mevlânâ?

The increased interest in Hz. Mevlânâ over the last decades is often attributed to the books published about him. In fact, it is the other way around: the publications are a product of the interest. The audience abroad already know about Hz. Mevlânâ. They not only read his works or the publications about him, they study his works in a systematic way. It is our deficiency not to read his works. The advanced technology of our time has made information quite accessible. Our fellow friends abroad bind together the spark in their hearts and love. To a certain extent, this is the business of mind. Yet, as Hz. Pîr set forth; there is a place that's out of reach for the mind. Only the heart can travel that part of the journey. I'm quite pleased to observe the build-up of intensive interest and curiosity in recent times. Coming back to the books, most of the publications in question are novels. I do think people should read them, but with the awareness that they are works of fiction. Then they must separately learn about the topic in a scholarly context. The fiction writers must also be sensible of their content, for utilizing the general frame of fiction wouldn't always justify presenting a random array of things in it.

Are you approached by authors who consult you in their process of writing?

It mostly happens after publication. Then I mark up the text to highlight the correct and mistaken elements. I don't know whether or not these inputs are taken into consideration. I performed many such reviews. I'm pleased to be of help. If only they could initiate these before publication. After my review, I at least suggest corrections to be made in the 2nd edition, which I think must be taken into account. I've read quite a number of film and theatre scripts, among which there were good projects. I shared my feedback with the writers. I'm not an expert on play scripts, but I think they must offer vivid, striking elements to engage and move the audience. So long as the script has a sound factual basis. There are some fabrications that, in the name of fiction, attribute baseless things to actual people. They use the names of people who lived and walked to *Haqq*. One must avoid such misdeeds.

What are the most common misconceptions about Hazrat Mevlânâ?

Everyone has a different personal view of Hz. Mevlânâ. What's most disquieting is that some people boil him down to be a humanist. Hz. Mevlânâ is beyond and above that. His love and respect encompasses all beings of creation, not just human. His thought is based on a genuine effort to seek and find a holy name of Allah in each created thing and apprcciate every being as a work of his Lord. Humanism, which is about love and respect for humans, therefore poses a far too limiting angle in understanding Hz. Mevlânâ.

Some people take the Mevlevî path for a philosophy, but it's not. It is a journey of the soul. It is a path to find knowledge on how to balance the inner and outer aspects of our lives.

That's what we learn from Hz. Mevlânâ's teachings. When people ask him: "If only we have a dervish lodge...", he replied: "The world is a dervish lodge." When they asked: "Who will enlighten us?" he said: "For that, you have Masnavî." This is the path we must follow. Every single happening in this world presents a message, a lesson to us; so long as we can see. We should know that Masnavî is a book of answers to many of our questions. But it does not open itself just as we open it. We need to have the contextual knowledge required to understand it. Then we will learn more from it. We will learn how to strike a balance between our inner and outer lives, and this will carry us further forward.

There are myriad of posts in social media with their content attributed to Hazrat Pîr. What would you like to say about that?

Hz. Mevlânâ took reference from only two sources: Quran and the hadith (words of Hz. Muhammad). He remarked: "Whoever carries a word of me apart from this, I am complainant of him, and I am complainant of those words too." Therefore he is complainant of whoever claims otherwise. This is important, as Allah says: "If you come to me with the wrong you did to me and ask forgiveness, I would forgive you. But if you come to me with the wrong you did to someone, then you must beg pardon of that servant of mine." You offended, slandered him, you spoke ill... "I am complainant of him, and I am complainant of those words too." is quite an important remark. Therefore, we have to take extra care. Much to our regret, in social media, there are contents ambiguously referencing Hz. Mevlânâ. Therefore it's hard to tell if they are valid. Content sharings of that kind must properly cite the specific name of the source work in use, with all the relevant details like Xth couplet of *Dîvân-ı Kebîr*, or Xth couplet of *Masnavî* Volume Y. Also, we must be considerate and avoid haphazard content sharings, for it's not quite right to share something you don't even know what it means or you don't genuinely believe.

What are your views on the initiatives to promote Hazrat Mevlânâ?

They are not sufficient. This is concerning the worldwide efforts; I'm not only speaking of Konya. We have to scale up and, at the same time, organize our efforts. While there are good individual initiatives, we can achieve much better if we can join forces and work together. In fact, we need professional support. Promotion is not our specialty. It goes beyond making posters and brochures, just as Hz. Mevlânâ is far from being just about Shab-i Arus. This place is swarmed with crowds all year round. We must, therefore, take our efforts to a new level. First, we have to know Hz. Mevlânâ well as the local people of Konya. We are talking about Hz. Pîr, the eponym of a school of wisdom that takes its source from the Quran, that is fresh and alive with an enduring influence since nearly 800 years.

Unfortunately, there are also those who protest him. Their misconceptions about Hz. Mevlânâ's messages are then presented as if Hz. Pîr's original thought. Yet, what leaks from us is nothing but what we harbor inside. What we can absorb is limited by our capacity. And what matters is to expand these limits and fill ourselves with beauty and goodness.

The number of Mevlevî groups are increasing. There are groups in Konya, in other Turkish cities and abroad. Are you, as the descendants of Hazrat Mevlânâ, informed about the activities of these groups, or do you only hear about them?

Unfortunately, the latter. I think these groups are ill-informed about the Mevlevî Order. Otherwise, they would have known that prior permission is sought for services done along this path. Much to our regret, in our own country, there are those whom we don't know, those who even proclaimed themselves as *sheikh* in Konya. As much as I hope they wouldn't harm our way, they do, because they distort and deform the tradition. Especially those who proclaim to be "a *semâzen*" do profound harm. They mistake *semâ* for a business, while *semâ is* a form of *dhikr* (Remembrance of Allah), a spiritual taste.

Every piece of clothing worn for *Âyin-i Şerif,* every single movement performed during the ritual, has a certain symbolic meaning. If whirling is performed without knowledge of these, then we can't call it *semâ.* It is rather - I can't find a better word- a "show." And these are growing in number every day. These practices are so wrong on so many levels... From glow-in-the-dark ritual gowns to the ones who claim to whirl on skateboards... We can't even use the term *semâ, or whirling* to describe what they do; they are just "turning." Sadly for everyone and even more for us, misconduct of that kind is quite prevalent. What's at stake is a nearly 800 years-old tradition, a path set by our forefathers. In the past, my ancestors strived to protect it in its pristine state. Today we try to keep up with their efforts.

As you know, with the stipulation of the Law of Dervish Lodges, the Mevlevî tradition has been entrusted to the

Republic of Turkey. Many people call us to account, questioning: "Why don't you mend these mistakes?" Those who sensibly share the implicated moral obligation expect us to take action. But we are not legally capable of doing anything. In any case, we are striving to do the best we can. For example, we prepare and present reports to the government authorities like the Presidency or the Ministry of Culture and Tourism. For nearly two decades, we update and re-present these reports at every relevant change of duty in these institutions, to work together with them.

As we mentioned before, our project named "Semâ and the Mevlevî Music" was recognized by UNESCO as a "Masterpiece of the Oral and Intangible Heritage of Humanity." Among the subsections of the project, there are: ensuring that *semâ* rituals are performed in the authentic form, re-opening *semâ* halls in the form of living museums upon completion of the needed repair and restoration works, taking care of the notable personages who were of service to the Mevlevî Path. The officials representing the Ministry of Culture and Tourism undersigned this, pledging to "Preserve these." Later, we have received a letter from UNESCO, asking us to follow-up with the Ministry on the implementation of the agreed actions regarding our project. Therefore, the project must be pursued per the contract, which we follow-up persistently. The Ministry issued several public mandates about the restrictions to apply regarding the places of semâ ritual. Yet these non-binding measures come without any sanction. So people carry on the misconduct. Therefore, taking the necessary measures for conservation of this heritage rests with the Ministry of Culture and Tourism, in other words, the government.

Could semâ rituals be performed in the grand performance halls of 10-15,000 people?

In the past, Âyin-i Şerif was not carried out outside the *semâhanes*, none of which were that capacious. It disconcerts the people who are cognizant of the essence of *semâ*. The entire semâ ritual delineates the process of disciplining the *nafs* (ego). It is performed as a form of *dhikr* (remembrance of Allah), a worship. A *semâzen* (whirler) steps on the ritual quarters always with ablution and without an unfulfilled obligatory prayer. He whirls by reciting the holy name Allah as a form of *dhikr*. It is a religious ceremony.

I believe that people will behave accordingly once they learn about these and that they will come to notice and mend their mistakes as they become informed.

Many people complain like: "They perform *semâ* here and there," but then they invite whirlers to perform in their private meetings. They have excuses like: "Well, ours is a religious meeting, religious wedding, night of henna etc." That's inconceivable. We will come to protect our heritage only as we become educated on the real meaning of *semâ*.

Believe me, in countries of Catholic majority; people watch *semâ* in tears. And when the ceremony is over, instead of leaving right away, they remain in their seats so as to breathe in the otherworldly atmosphere a little more. That was even the case in Vatican. I hope that people of my land will also perceive the essence of the semâ ritual and dispel this spiritual pollution.

What would you like to say about Shab-i Arus?

Shab-i Arus, as you know, is the day when Hazrat Mevlânâ walked to *Haqq* and reunited with his beloved Allah. On that, he said: "I am going to the beloved." Death is not an end; it is a passage to the spiritual realm from the material world, which is not to be feared. The body, which is considered to perish, is only making its way back to the soil- where it came from.

In the past, semâ rituals were customarily performed across all the *Mevlevî Houses* in the evenings of *Shab-i Arus*. This is no longer in place since the closure of the *Mevlevî Houses* (like all other kinds of Sufi lodges and schools) per the Law of Dervish Lodges in 1925. But until then, the Quran recitations and semâ rituals in the evening had always been part of each *Shab-i Arus*. Because that's what Hz. Mevlânâ had asked. You know, he had even asked the visitors of his tomb to bring along tambourines. He had asked people to think of it as a wedding night, "the night of my reunion with Allah, the greatest beloved of all" and wished for a ceremony of that kind. So the commemorations in the *Mevlevî Houses* were like that until their closure. *Mevlevî*s steered clear of legally banned acts and pursued all their practices within the law.

Then in the 1940s, they started to organize commemorative events on December 17th (the day Hz. Mevlânâ walked to *Haqq*)- first with conferences and in later years with concerts of tasawwuf music as well. In the 1950s the government allowed for *semâ* rituals, but with less emphasis on the religious aspects. Today, the commemorative events in Konya draw people from all over the world -not just Turkey. And Hz. Mevlânâ is memorialized not only in Konya but in all corners of the world.

Which aspects of Hazrat Mevlânâ, among many others, would deserve particular highlighting in our times? Could you share your perspective in a nutshell?

Hz. Mevlânâ is an eminent Turkish-Islamic scholar. For us, the Turkish people, he is also a revered friend of Allah (*wali*). For me, as a grandchild, he conjures up an image of a loving father and grandfather. We can find confirming notes in the works of his son Sultan Veled in Sipehsâlâr, and in Eflâkî's Manaqib al-Ârifin. Hz. Mevlânâ was a devoted Muslim, abiding its obligations like fasting and daily prayers. Hz. Mevlânâ was not just a humanist; he was a Sufi master; he was a *wali*. In that respect, let him directly answer the question: "What is indispensable to you? Whom do you love the most?"

"As long as I live, I am the slave of the Quran; I am the ground of chosen Mohammed's way.
Whoever carries a word of me apart from this, I am complainant of him, and I am complainant of those words too."[20]

We must view Hz. Mevlânâ's works through the lens of this quatrain, which holds the key for us catch the spirit and grasp the true meaning of his words. The scholars of this field call the Masnavî a Tafsir of Quran. Hz. Pîr presented us with a view of Islam, which is centered on divine love (*love of Allah*). He, who said: "All kinds of love are bridges to divine love," alludes to *love of Allah* each time he says "love." His works are centered on humanity. But his thought also reflects the notion of love and respect for all created beings, conveyed through a variety of poems and parables in his works. And essentially, Hz. Pîr taught us how to attain inner peace,

20 Translator's Note: English translation by Feyzi Halıcı is taken from http://mevlana.net/mevlana.html.

recognize our worth, and stay at peace with ourselves, how to educate ourselves and walk in the guiding path of the perfected human (*insan-ı kâmil*). In his books, he showed us the way to become loving and forbearing humans, grateful in awareness of all the tangible and intangible blessings that Allah bestowed on ourselves; he guided us to be the ones who know how to act in the face of adversity.

The following, Hz. Mevlânâ's advice to his son, Bahaddin Veled, indicates his spiritual and worldly viewpoints:

Bahaeddin! Should you wish to be in Heaven forever, be a friend to everyone.
Cherish no grudge in your heart,
Demand not extra nor be extra; Be like ointment and candle, not a needle.
Should you wish no evil from anyone,
Speak not of evil, Nor preach of evil, Nor think evil!
Should you speak of a man in goodwill, you will always rejoice,
And that joy is Heaven itself.
Should you speak of a man in hostility, you will always despair.
And this is Hell itself.
As soon as you ponder friends, flowers will bloom in your heart's garden, filling it with roses and basil.
As soon as you ponder foes, your heart's garden will be filled with thorns and serpents.
Your heart will grow tired, and you will lie idle.
All prophets and saints did likewise, reflecting their character outwards.
Fellow human beings, overwhelmed by their beautiful demeanor, voluntarily and happily followed their path.[21]

21 Translator's note: Original text: (Manaqib al-Ârifin by Eflâkî, Vol: II). English translation is taken from http://mevlana.net/works.html.

How do you feel when you are in Hazrat Mevlânâ's tomb?

I feel the warmth of a grandfather; it feels like home. Regardless of how crowded it is. All that matters is to know why you are there. I greet him, recite the surah al-Fâtiha and pray for the whole world. There, I feel like I sit by my grandfather. I direct all my prayers to Allah. For the sake of Hz. Mevlânâ, I pray to Allah for my knowledge and services to abound, so that I can share these with others.

When it comes to Hazrat Shams...

Hazrat Shams was another worthy scholar. He was an admirer of *Haqq* and a perfected *wali* (friend of Allah), seeking to commune with a companion on his own level. Ever since childhood, he had been a dervish ecstatically immersed in divine love with a free mind and soul. Endowed with sight of the unseen, he had no one to share his experiences that lie beyond the grasp of ordinary people. So he prays: "My dear Allah, give me a true companion to pass on my wisdom so that he becomes the one to enlighten people." As he hears: "What will you give in return?" He responds without hesitation: "My head!" Then he's inspired by Allah that his companion is Muhammed Celâleddîn, the son of the Sultânü'l-Ulemâ of Balkh who lives in Anatolia. That's how Shams travels to Konya, and the two meet there. Their close friendship is that of the hearts, such that they spend days sitting in absolute silence through which they exchange heavenly wisdom. It is such an interaction that, in their own words, they had interchangeably been the master and the disciple. Yet, people fail to understand and one day Hz. Shams flees away.

Photograph 54: Inside the tomb of Hazrat Mevlânâ.

Hz. Mevlânâ, in his deep grief, secludes himself from all friends and writes many of his verses which we read in *Dîvân-ı Kebîr*. The instigators of this unfavorable situation express remorse and a group led by Mevlânâ's son Sultan Veled goes to Damascus and brings back Shams. Nevertheless, jealousy arises once again, and Shams, this time, suddenly disappears altogether. Even though his tomb is assumed to be in Konya, whether he deserted the city or was murdered still remains a mystery. We can somehow relate to the experience of having someone to share a lot of things without words. Sometimes it is only a glance. Sometimes a bird's song reveals the answer after you search volumes of books.

You said, "Hazrat Mevlânâ presented us with a view of Islam, which is centered on divine love (love of Allah)." Hz. Pîr has a saying: "Our mother is love, our father is love, we are born of love, we are love. All kinds of love are bridges to the divine love." Which love is meant here?

Aşk (love) is originally an Arabic word that means "ivy." In the most general sense, *Aşk* and another Turkish synonym *Sevi* stand for an attachment, fondness, a passionate longing for something. We can talk about two kinds of love: worldly and otherworldly, corresponding to metaphorical love (*Aşk-ı mecâzi*) and divine love (*Aşk-ı ilâhî*). The first one is related to worldly pleasures. As for Hz. Mevlânâ and other Sufi thinkers, this kind of love is transient and mundane.

Mevlânâ tells us to follow the path of *Aşk-ı ilâhî*, which is the love felt towards Allah. He says: "Love is the attribute of God, who has no need of anyone. To be in love with other than Him is metaphorical love, a fleeting desire."[22] In other words, no one and nothing but Allah is real and eternal. And love for anything that is bound to perish is an illusion.

The Quran verse that says: "Everything will perish except His own face"[23] serves as proof.

"Love feeds on faith. It neither seeks bread, nor strives for life."

Hz. Mevlânâ describes real love as such. He says that divine love gives us joy and comfort, that a life without love doesn't count. Just as a person cherishes his union with a worldly love, true lovers of Allah rejoice when they reach out to *Haqq* in the spiritual sense. It is like dying before death. As for Mevlânâ, this kind of love is beyond the comprehension of the intellectual mind. Trying to write about this love would crack pens. Divine love resembles a chain hanging from the skies, which would carry the lover to the beloved if he clings to it and climb the way in good faith.

"My love is more pristine than clear water. To me, this play of love is not ill-gotten, for it is far from lust. Love shapes and reshapes others, makes them pass from one state to another. Yet my love is not transient. And my imperishable beloved is immortal."

"Those who fell because of lust, could never rise again." That's how Hazrat Mevlânâ puts it.

22 Translator's Note: English translation is taken from: "Can, Şefik, *Fundamentals of Rumis Thought*, ed. and transl.: Zeki Sarıtoprak, Tughra Books, New Jersey, 2008".

23 Surat al-Qasas 28/88. English translation by Yusuf Ali: http://corpus.quran.com/translation.jsp?chapter=28&verse=88.

As you know, lust means an extreme desire for things. Here, Hz. Pîr suggests that excessive desires would drag us to a lower state of being. Blessings blindfold, gratitude awakens. We must praise Allah every moment for all the beauties around us and give thanks for all the blessings. These are quite important. Everyone says: "You always have a smile on your face." Because I choose to see the glass half full rather than half empty, and I feel grateful for that. Praise to Allah. I am aware of the gift my Lord bestowed on me. Building on that, I spend efforts to fill the other side. That's the whole point. Unfortunately, the opposite seems to hold for the modern-day people, who ruin themselves in vain for the empty side. This is one of the points I underline in my conversations with young people: What are you gifted with? Think of it; consider what's at hand, not what's lacking. And express your heartfelt gratitudes to Allah for that. Converse with Allah, for prayer, means a conversation. Let your prayer be: "My dear Allah. Praises to you. I cherish all your blessings. Thank you." Then you can own and pursue your wishes, perhaps setting goals and working on attaining whatever you lack for the moment.

Some people argue: "How is it possible to turn a blind eye to the bad things in life?"

We have to appreciate the good things first, and it is also possible to change certain things- like making good out of bad. Hz. Mevlânâ says: "There is hope, don't go the way of hopelessness. There are suns, do not go into the darkness."[24]

24 English translation is taken from: "Kenan Rıfâî, *Listen (Commentary on the Spiritual Couplets of Mevlana Rumi)*, Trans.: Victoria Rowe Holbrook, Fons Vitae Publishing, İstanbul, 2011".

Looking on the dark side would get us nowhere. And despair drags us down into its vicious spiral. We have our Lord. Allah created humans to be loved and known. Likewise, the creation of the universe is a present to humanity. All for what? To find out the truth, we must know ourselves. He who knows his self, knows his Lord. Isn't it? So we must first learn: Who are we? Why are we here on earth? We all have so many gifts that make us who we are... We must examine ourselves. I share these notions with young people. I suggest them to reflect on these questions through a process of writing, which helps to catch fleeting thoughts.

I believe everything happens for a reason, and moaning about the seemingly misfortunate events is just futile. It is natural to feel shaken at first. I've also dealt with ups and downs in my life. In the face of certain events, I also reacted like: "How could this happen to me?" But I was quick to move on and ask: "What can I learn from that?" The mishaps in our lives begin to serve us once we make sense out of them, carrying us to higher levels in our development. This is the whole point. In fact, every single moment, Allah blesses us with gifts. If only we could see. All that matters is to unveil the gift that marks who you are and set out on a path to do the best to become the best version of yourself.

This reminds me of this parable about the ant who decided to embark on a Hajj pilgrimage. When challenged: "With this pace, you won't live long enough to make it!" The ant said: "So be it. That would make me one who died on the way." We need to speak more of goodness. Today, modern science and medicine recognize the phenomenon of "energy." Like attracts like; therefore we need to develop a positive mindset and speak of good, to redound positive vibes. I'm not saying we should ignore the adversities. We must acknowledge them with the intent to seek out ways to resolve them.

Masnavî abounds with tales. One of my favorites among those is the one that my grandmother often used to tell us. A practical way to convey a message. A woman is boiling chickpeas. When one chickpea jumps out of the pot, she pushes it back into the hot water with her slotted spoon and says: "I'm not doing this to hurt you. This is for you to gain taste and eventually become a human."

For me, there were two things to take away from this tale:

First, a chickpea literally becomes a human cell after it is cooked and eaten. The second, the difficulties in life are there to transform us into mature beings, to transform our perspective of life. Whatever we dislike turns out to serve us in that direction. The school of life, with some difficult lessons to take and exams to pass, poses a good analogy in that respect. Perspective really matters. Take, for instance, this the window in my room: you may look at it, or look out of it. The former shows us a dirty pane of glass wetted by raindrops, true? But the latter shows us the tomb of Hz. Mevlânâ, a beautiful view.

What is your favorite ghazal among the works of Hazrat Mevlânâ?

I think the one that begins with "come over" is the most up-to-date.

"Come, come, get closer. Till when is this banditry going to continue? Since you are I and I am you, what is this "us and them"? We are God's holy light; we are God's mirror. So why

are we struggling with each other? Why is one light running away from another light so much? We, all humans, are gathered like a body in the being of a mature person. But why are we squint-eyed? Although we are limbs of the same body, why do the rich look down on the poor? Why does the right hand look down on the left hand of the same body?

We, all humans, are in reality all one essence. Our minds are one, and our heads are one.

But we have seen one as two because of the curvature of the heavens. Come, liberate yourself from this selfishness and reconcile with everybody and be nice to people. As long as you are in you, you are a grain, a particle. But when you mix and unite with others, then you become an ocean, a mine.

Every human carries the same soul, but the bodies are in hundreds of thousands. Similarly, there are countless almonds in the world, but there is the same oil in each of them. There are many tongues and dialects in this world, but the meaning of all of them is the same. Water put in different containers unites when the containers are broken and starts to flow together as one stream. If you understand that unity, tawhid, means, if you attain unity and if you rip and throw away meaningless words and thoughts, the spirit sends news to those whose hearts' eyes are open and tells them the truth."[25]

Let's end our questions with one on your father Celâleddin Bâkır Çelebi.

25 Translator's Note: Original text: (Dîvân-ı Kebîr by Mevlânâ, Vol: VI). English translation is taken from: "Can, Şefik, *Fundamentals of Rumi's Thought*, Trans.: Zeki Sarıtoprak, Cüneyt Eroğlu, The Light Inc., New Jersey, 2004".

My father worked and exchanged ideas from time to time with Abdülbâki Gölpınarlı, Şefik Can, Hüseyin Top and (his son-in-law) Ahmed Güner Sayar. During these studies, his wife Güzîde Hanım was his greatest support. Sometimes, while preparing for conferences, he would excitedly share passages he came across in *Masnavî* or *Dîvân-ı Kebîr* with his wife, his children, and grandchildren; he would come out of his study and exclaim, "Güzîde! Listen... *Suphânallah* (Good God!) What an amazing word!" Aside from some occasional flashes of temper he had while carrying out his responsibilities in earnest, he radiated love with his witty and cheerful personality. He was a modern man both in appearance and thought, who kept himself up to date on the latest technological and other developments of the time. It is worth noting that he was among the first computer users in Turkey.

Meanwhile, he rendered many of the aforementioned services while suffering a heart condition and despite all the doctors' recommendations for him to pursue a slow-paced, calm life. Neither the heart attacks nor the by-pass operation could stop him from serving in the way of his ancestor, from disseminating the age-old teachings and wisdom of his forefathers. Yet, one day his heart gave in to the overflowing love he had, and on the evening of April 13, 1996, he departed the room of this life and passed into the realm of eternal life. After the funeral prayers at the Teşvikiye Mosque in Istanbul on April 16 and Sultan Selim Mosque in Konya on April 17, he was carried -literally on an ocean of shoulders- to Üçler Cemetery, where he now rests in the section of our family.

"As long as I live, I am the slave of the Quran;
I am the ground of chosen Mohammed's way.

Whoever carries a word of me apart from this,
I am complainant of him, and I am complainant of those words too."

Inspired by Hz. Mevlânâ's words above, he had written a poem named "Forever like Hz. Mevlânâ", the last part of which was then inscribed to his gravestone upon the wish of my mother Güzîde Çelebi.

When my soul re-unites with Allah, on the command "Return",
When my body turns into soil,
With every fiber of my being, dead or alive, forever,
I will remain to be the dust under the feet of Hz. Muhammed.

Photograph 55: The gravestone of Celâleddin Bâkır Çelebi.

My father Celâleddin Bâkır Çelebi had a life spent in serving his lineage, his nation, and religion. In other words, for my father, being a Mevlevî Turkish Muslim was a priceless gift; therefore he worked to share it with everyone regardless of language, religion, and race.

I would like to end my words by praying: As we represent the Çelebi family's living strands on earth today, may Allah bless us and our future generations with the gift to continue serving this way.

GLOSSARY

This section contains a list of specific traditional terms that appear in*italicized* form throughout the book. Neither the Mevlevî tradition nor the Turkish culture could be summarized in such a brief compilation. Yet we hope this section would humbly guide and assist the reader (of this English-translated edition), who is, in a way, taking a journey across cultures by reading it. Far from being a standalone scholarly work, this section is rather a compilation based on the works of reputable sources that are listed at the end (references are explicitly marked with numbers and denoted in quotation marks). Presented in three broad categories, the terms appear in Turkish, as well as in Turkish-English or Persian-English or Arabic-English transliterated versions (depending on the word's origin).

I. TITLES AND EXPRESSIONS IN TURKISH CULTURE, INCLUDING THE ONES SPECIFIC TO THE MEVLEVÎ TRADITION

Abla / Sister: Literal meaning: elder sister.

A generic address form not only used for siblings but also for elder or senior females. It could be used as a standalone reference or be used after the person's name.

Ağa / Agha: A traditional male title, signifying power generally related to land ownership, widespread in the traditional as well as modern rural culture. It could be used as a standalone reference or be used after the person's name.

Ağabey / Brother: Literal meaning: elder brother.

A generic address form not only used for siblings but also for elder or senior males. It could be used as a standalone reference or be used after the person's name.

Bey / Mr., or Sir: A generic address form used for men as a common address of respect and formality (both in the modern and traditional Turkish culture). It is used after the first name or, in some cases, the person's full name.

Çelebi / Chalabi, or Chelebi: Literal meaning: well-mannered, educated person.

An honorific title in the Mevlevî tradition. It could be used as a standalone reference or be used after the person's name.

When used in capital letters (Makam Çelebisi, Maqam Chalabi or Chalabi Master), it signifies the title for the hereditary leader of the Mevlevî Order, elected from among the lineage of Hz. Mevlânâ. (1)

Chelebi (*Tur.* Çelebi), Master (*Tur.* Çalab), Mawla (*Tur.* Mevlâ) are interchangeably used for God/Lord but also used to call masters.

Dede / Mevlevî Elder: Literal meaning: grandfather.

A generic address form nor only used for grandfather but also used to address elder men.

In the Mevlevî culture, Dede specifically refers to a spiritual rank given to a dervish once he completes a certain type of education, fulfilling a number of requirements.

It also refers to Mevlevî elders and notables.

Efendi / Affandi, Master: An address form used for men of rank in a particular field. It could be used as a standalone reference or be used after the person's name or other honorific titles.

Gazi / Ghazi: Title of honor awarded to people of significant military achievements, often denoting people of high rank in the military.

Hacı / Hadji, or Hajji: Pilgrim. Often adopted as an honorific title preceding the name of Muslims who have made the pilgrimage to Mecca (hajji for men, hajjah for women). (4)

Hâfız / Hafiz, or Hafez: *Hâfız* (or Hafez) means 'one who has memorized the Quran. (5)

Hanım / Mrs., Madam: A generic address form used for women as a common address of respect and formality (both in the modern and traditional Turkish culture). It is used after the first name or, in some cases, the person's full name.

Hanımefendi / Lady: An address form used for women as an address of respect and formality (both in the modern and traditional Turkish culture), it connotes a highly respected woman. It is used after the first name or, in some cases, the person's full name.

Hatun / Khatun, Matron: A traditional female title generally used to address women of rank or seniority. It is used after the person's name.

Hazret (Abbr.: Hz.) / Hazrat, or Hadrat: Literal meaning: presence.

"An honorific which precedes the names of holy personages. It means, 'the venerable, his excellency.'" (1)

Hoca / Hodja, Teacher, Professor: Literal meaning: teacher.

A traditional title used for scholars or teachers. Hodja (*Tur.*

Hoca) often refers to religious scholars, while Professor (*Tur.* Hoca) is commonly used for teachers in any kind of discipline. It could be used as a standalone reference or be used after the person's name.

Paşa / Pasha: An address of respect for men.

Turkish abbreviation of Persian padishah, "sovereign" (Arabic basha). Title of honor awarded in the thirteenth to nineteenth centuries mostly to generals, governors, and viziers in the Ottoman administration, rarely to religious officials or women. After the mid-nineteenth-century Tanzimat reforms it was given to the highest four grades in the civil and military hierarchies, and from 1923 to 1934 only to soldiers. (4)

Pîr / Pir: Literal meaning: old man, elder.

"A translation into Persian of the Arabic word, "shaykh," which has the same literal meaning, but means a Sufi elder--a spiritual guide, teacher, master.

This word is also used to mean the founder of a Sufi order. For Mevlevîs, their "Pîr" in this sense is Mawlânâ Jalâlu 'd-dîn Rûmî." (1)

Şerif / Sharif, or Sherif: An honorific title that refers to the descendants of Hz. Muhammad from his grandson Hz. Hasan ibn Ali.

Seyyid, or Seyid / Sayyid, Sayid, Syed: An honorific title that refers to the descendants of Hz. Muhammad from his grandson Hz. Hasan ibn Ali.

Sultan / Sultan: A traditional title that's often used as a male or female title to address royal status. It's also used for a person who is a master in a certain field.

II. HOLY NAMES AND REFERENCES RELATED TO ALLAH

Allah / God: Generic meaning: "The name of God in Islam" is a common description provided in dictionaries.

Although the closest term in English may be God, the word Allah in Islam has different connotations.

Hak / Haqq: One of the holy names of Allah.

The true, the real, that which is exactly opposite to batil, the unreal, the transitory. Al-*Haqq* is thus supremely the title of God in the Qur'an.

Rab / Lord: Literal meaning: Lord, master, owner, teacher. When used with a definite article and a capitalized initial, Ar-*Rabb* (The Lord), it denotes one of the holy names of Allah in Islam.

III. OTHER TERMS

Âdab, or Âdap / Manners, Etiquette, Discipline: Literal meaning: refined manners, etiquette, proper conduct, courtesy, discipline

Meaning in Sufism: the modes of conduct and discipline of the dervishes toward their spiritual guide (sheikh), toward each other, and toward other people in general. (1)

It should be kept in mind too that sufis went as far as to say al-tasawwuf kulluhu adab - 'Sufism, all of it, is acts of courtesy.' (7)

Âsitâne / Mevlevî House, Dervish Lodge: Literal or generic meaning: threshold; also means a saint's tomb.

Meaning in Turkish Sufism: A large dervish center.

In the Mevlevî Order: Among the Mevlevî Houses, the âsitânes were the only centers where new Mevlevîs could undergo the 1001 day retreat and training. (1)

Aşçı Dede / Chief Cook, or Chief of Kitchen: In the Mevlevî tradition, the "chief cook" was the chief trainer of dervishes; he was also responsible for collecting revenues, managing expenses, and hosting guests. (1)

Âyin / Ritual: Literal meaning: Ceremony, custom, ritual.

Meaning in Sufism: The ritual of a Sufi order, performed on certain days.

In the Mevlevî tradition, it is also the name for a musical composition which is played and sung for the Whirling Prayer Ceremony (*semâ*); the sung parts are usually from Mevlânâ's Dîvân: verses from ghazals or rubâ`îs. (1)

Âyinhan / Ayinkhan: "A musician who sings the vocal parts of the composition, which consists of verses chosen by the composer (mainly from Mawlânâ's Dîvân)" (1)

Âyin-i Cem / Ayin-i Cem, Ayin-i Jem: Literal meaning: Ceremony or ritual (Âyin) of gathering together (Cem).

While the term Âyin-i Cem refers to a basic worship in Alevism, it refers to a different ritual in the Mevlevi tradition:

"an informal all-night Mevlevî ritual in Konya to commemorate the anniversary of Hz. Mevlânâ's death (according to the Muslim lunar calendar). An abbreviated version of the Whirling Prayer (*semâ*) was done in which the dervishes turned slowly wearing the black cloak (khirqa) (no tanûra or opening the arms), without stopping between the salâms. The Na`t-ı Sharîf and the Dawr-i Waladî were not done. This informal ceremony could also be done at other times and occasions, in which a monetary gift was usually provided for the special meal and desserts." (1)

Âyin-i Şerif (Semâ) / Ayin-i Sharif, Sema: Literal meaning: "Noble Ceremony."

Meaning in the Mevlevî Tradition: "The term both refers to the Whirling Prayer Ceremony (see: Semâ), and to the title of the musical compositions (in four sections) for the Semâ." (1)

Dergâh / Dervish Lodge, or Sufi Center: Literal meaning: "Dar-gah means door-place, gate-place."

"Dergah (also: *tekke*) is the generic name of a sufi center, a place where dervishes would meet and do prayer-chanting (*zikr*) and to receive spiritual instruction from the teacher. These were usually humble buildings, though some which were well-funded were large enough to contain separate cells for the dervishes to live in, a kitchen, and an attached mosque." (1)

The sufi centers of the Mevlevî Order have been in the form of Mevlevî Houses (see: *Mevlevîhane*), which were divided into two kinds: *Âsitâne* and *Zâviye.* (2)

Derviş / Dervish, or Darwish, or Sufi: Literal meaning: "beggar at the door"

It is a generic term that refers to sufi mystics in Islam. (See also: *Tasawwuf, Tarîkat*)

Destâr-ı Şerif / Dastar-ı Sharif: Dastar is the sash which is wrapped around a turban. When the dastar is wrapped around the traditional Mevlevi hat (*sikke*), it is called *Destâr-ı şerif.* "In the Mevlevî tradition, it is primarily the shaykhs and Masnavi teachers who are permitted to wear *Destâr-ı şerif.*" (1)

Devr / Dawr: Literal meaning: circling, revolving, spinning.

"The sufi practice of doing Zikr while whirling" (1)

Devr-i Veledî / Dawr-i Waladi: "In the Whirling Prayer Ceremony (semâ), a ritual circumambulation of three rounds said to be in honor of Mawlânâ's son, Sultân Walad. It precedes the whirling prayer." (1)

Edep / Manner, Self-discipline, Decency: Literal meaning: Singular version of the term adab.

Erkân / Method, or Discipline and Conduct: Literal meaning: way, method, rules of conduct applied in a certain discipline.

The Mevlevî life is based on "adab and erkan" (discipline and rules of conduct). (1) (2)

Gülbang / Gol-bang: Literal meaning: "sound of rose"

"A sufi and Mevlevî term for a prayer blessing holy personages of the past who are part of the Mevlevî lineage intoned in solemn Persian by a leader following a meal, the semâ, and on other occasions." (1)

Hâmûşân / Mevlevî Cemetery: Literal meaning: the ones in silence.

In the Mevlevî culture, it is believed that there is no death but going silent. Therefore, Mevlevî cemeteries are called "the ones in silence".

Himmet / Himmat, Benevolence: *"Himmat*, the fourth pillar of sufi synergy, is the reciprocating grace and favor of the saints that come from one's hard work. Service is the entirety of your work on the path. You cry out "*himmat*!" and your *sheikh* will answer you, "*khidmat* (service)!" Work and strive, *himmat* will come." (3)

Hırka / Khirka, Dervish Coat, Mevlevi Ritual Cardigan: "A type of dervish's cloak. In the Mevlevi Whirling Prayer Ceremony (semâ), it is a long blackcloak with very long sleeves and no collar or buttons." (1)

Within the context of *semâ*, hırka symbolizes the tomb of the dervish's ego. (2)

Hû: Third-person singular pronoun that is used to a reference to Allah.

"In sufism the Name of God, which indicates the Divine Essence of God is understood to be Hû." (1)

Kelime-i Şahâdet / Kalimah Shahadat: Kalimah (word) Shahadat (obtaining direct evidence for something through being a witness) is a declaration: "I bear witness that there is no God but Allah, and Hazrat Mohammad is Allah's servant and messenger." Reciting Kalimah Shahadat is a precondition of becoming a Muslim.

Kırmızı Post / Red Sheepskin: "In the Whirling Prayer Ceremony (semâ), it is a red sheep skin upon which the shaykh stands and sits. It can be interpreted symbolically in a number of ways, some of which are as follows. The red color symbolizes the manifestation of God to the prophets and saints. It also symbolizes the sunset (at the time of Mawlânâ's death), as well as a symbol of Shams (the Sun) of Tabrizi. It is traditionally placed in front of the mihrâb, indicating the direction of Mecca. Therefore, when the shaykh, semâzens, and musicians bow toward the *pôst* at the beginning and end of the Ceremony, They are bowing in respect to Mawlânâ, as well as toward Mecca." (1)

Kudüm / Qudum: Literal meaning: drum

One of the instruments played during the Whirling Prayer Ceremony (semâ):

"a small double drum played with small sticks" (1)

Lohusa: Lohusa signifies, in Turkish tradition, the first forty days of postpartum.

Makam Çelebisi / Maqam Chalabi, Chalabi Master, Chief Master: Hereditary leader of the Mevlevî Order (see also: *Çelebi*, or *Chalabi*)

Matbâh-ı Şerîf / Matbah-ı Sharif, Kitchen of the Mevlevi Houses: In the Mevlevî tradition, matbah is not only a kitchen but also a place where the disciples' initial education of 1001 days (period of sufferance) was finalised.

Medrese / Madrasa: Theological University, also known as Madrasa

Mevlevîhâne / Mevlevî House, or Mevlevî Center: "A building or complex (dergâh) where Mevlevîs engage in activities involving this sufi order" (1) The Mevlevî Houses have been divided into two kinds, which vary in terms of size and functionality- see: *Âsitâne* and *Zâviye.* (2)

Meydân-ı Şerif / Meydan-ı Sharif: Literal meaning of meydan : arena, quarter.

Meydan-ı sharif is the ritual quarter, the room where the traditional Mevlevî ceremonies, like semâ take place.

Meydancı Dede: The dede responsible for the general organization of a Mevlevî lodge. (1)

Mutrib / Musician: Literal meaning: musician.

"In the Whirling Prayer Ceremony (semâ), one of the instrumental musicians or singers" (1)

Na't, Naat / Eulogy: Literal meaning: praise.

"It is an eulogy, usually in the form of a poem (often sung), especially in honor of the Prophet Muhammad" (1)

Naathân / Naatkhan, Reciter of Na't-ı Sharif: In the Whirling Prayer Ceremony (semâ), the musician who sings the Na`t-ı Sharîf, in praise of the Prophet Muhammad. (1)

Na't-ı Şerif / Na't-ı Sharif, Noble Eulogy: Literal meaning: noble praise.

"Sema ceremony begins with an eulogy, called Na't-ı Şerif, to the Prophet Muhammad." (1)

Nev-niyâz / Novice Mevlevi Disciple: Literal meaning: new supplicant

"The name given to a Mevlevî novice during his 1001-day training; also the name given to someone newly initiated as a disciple (murîd) and beginning whirler (semâzen)" (1)

Ney / Reed Flute: "A reed flute, with nine holes (a thumb hole, six finger holes, and the top and bottom openings)." "It is played especially in Mevlevi ceremonies and gatherings, and is the main symbol in the first eighteen lines of the Mathnawi (Masnavi)." (1) Ney is one of the instruments played during semâ.

Neyzen / Reed Flute Player: "A reed flute, with nine holes (a thumb hole, six finger holes, and the top and bottom openings)." "It is played especially in Mevlevi ceremonies and gatherings, and is the main symbol in the first eighteen lines of the Mathnawi (Masnavi)." (1) Ney is one of the instruments played during semâ.

Niyâz / Supplication: Literal meaning: "Neediness, supplication."

"Means the neediness of a dervish before God. This is a major teaching of Mawlânâ's: that since Divine Mercy responds to true neediness, the dervish must increase his or her neediness in order to receive Divine blessings and greater nearness to God (see Masnavi II: 3274). This term was also used to mean a gift humbly offered by someone to a Mevlevî dervish, dede, shaykh, or to the Mevlevî center." (1)

Niyâz Penceresi / Niyaz Window, Window of Supplication: "This refers to a window facing the tomb of a dervish, where people may stand, raise their hands and pray the Fâtiha, and ask for the departed holy person's intercession with God (granted by the permission of God). The window gives the people access to the tomb when the door of the building (that contains the tomb) is locked." (1)

Postnişin / Postnishin, Posthesnin: "In the Whirling Prayer Ceremony (semâ), the Mevlevi shaykh who stands and sits on the red sheep skin (pôst) and who is the leader of the Ceremony. The term is also used for the Mevlevi shaykh, who is the head of a lodge (dergâh, tekke). In the Whirling Prayer Ceremony (semâ), the pôst-neshîn symbolizes the presence of Mawlânâ Jalâluddîn Rûmî." (1)

Semâ / Sema: Literal meaning: "hearing, audition (not related to the Arabic word, samâ, meaning sky)"

"The Whirling Prayer Ceremony" (1)

"Semâ came to symbolize Mevlevi Order for it is the oldest ritual of the Order. Accompanied by music and systemized by certain rules, the "whirling" act, which is, in essence, a form of dhikr (Tur. *zikir*, Eng. remembrance of Allah), a form of pray for the Mevlevi dervishes. Sema ritual symbolizes the journey of the vassal and its several stages where the vassal first purified his, re-united with Allah, and returned to vassalage as a perfect human.

In sufism, semâ was originally a spiritual exercise done in sufi gatherings (beginning in Baghdad, several centuries before Mawlânâ's time), involving spontaneous physical movement and dance-like motions inspired by listening to recitations from the Qur'ân, sufi poetry, or sufi music and songs. The dervishes would listen as if hearing the voice of God, the "music" of the spheres, or the "sound" from the primordial state of Unity before the creation-- and they would enter ecstatic spiritual states of consciousness. In the Mevlevi tradition, this became formalized into a ritual of disciplined whirling called the Whirling Prayer Ceremony (semâ), accompanied by music composed by Mevlevi musicians over the centuries, during which Persian and Turkish poetry is sung (composed mainly by Rumi, his son, and grandson). Nowadays, the original meaning of the term has been forgotten in Turkey, so that it only means "whirling." (For example: "There is Semâ tonight" can mean the full or abbreviated Mevlevi Whirling Prayer Ceremony, or just semazens whirling in costume while musicians play hymns; likewise, "He did Semâ" can mean that a semâzen whirled in the Ceremony, or that he whirled alone.)" (1)

Aside from the information provided throughout the book, further information on the details of the ritual can be found in: http://mevlanafoundation.com/mevlevi_order_en.html

Semâhâne / Whirling Hall: Literal meaning: "house of audition."

"In the Mevlevi tradition, this is a building or hall designed for the Whirling Prayer Ceremony (semâ)" (1)

Semâzen / Semazen, Whirler in Sema: "Someone trained to be a "whirler" in the Whirling Prayer Ceremony (semâ). The semazen whirls with the left foot solidly on the floor; the right foot touches the floor after a complete circle, pointing toward the center of the circle, and stepping according to the beat of the music; the arms are outstretched and held upward; the right hand is opened to the sky, and the left hand is turned downward; the eyelids are narrowed, and the gaze is upon the left thumb; the head is turned leftward (the direction of the heart), and bent toward the upheld right arm; the inward concentration has a spiritual focus on the heart, the mental repetition of the zikr, "Al-lâh, Al-lâh" with each step and rotation of the whirling, and an awareness that God is All-Present within the "Ka`ba of the heart" and in all directions: "Whichever way you turn, there is the Face of God" (Qur'ân 2: 115). During the Ceremony, the semazens also move around the hall in a circle while whirling and then whirl in place during the fourth section (salâm). Although the whirling is dance-like, it should not be called a "dance" or "dancing" because it is a form of prayerful concentration on the Name of God (Allâh) and not a way of experiencing physical excitement or pleasure, nor is it a performance intended to impress viewers." (See: *semâ*) (1)

Semâzenbaşı / Semazenbashı, Head of the Semazens: "-bashı (Tur. *-başı*) is a Turkish suffix, indicating leadership positions, such as semazenbashı (head of the semazens)" (1)

Sikke / Sikke, Traditional Mevlevi Hat: Sikke is the tall conical hat in the Mevlevi tradition.

In the Whirling Prayer Ceremony (semâ), sikke symbolizes the tombstone of the dervish's nafs (ego). (2)

Şeb-i Arûs / Seb-i Arus, or Shab-i Arus: Literal meaning: wedding night.

"The term refers to the night when Mawlânâ Jalâluddîn Rûmî died (and became "wedded" to God, the Beloved). A special Whirling Prayer Ceremony (semâ) is observed on the anniversary of this night (December 17 on the Western solar calendar, since 1953, when the Turkish government gave permission for the first time since organized sufism was made illegal in 1925). However, the event was celebrated in previous centuries according to the Islamic lunar calendar). It is traditional in sufism to celebrate the "wedding" of a great sufi, on the (lunar calendar) anniversary of death." (1)

Şerbet-i Velâdet / Birth Sherbet, Traditional Birth Drink: Traditional sweet fruit drinks served a short while after the birth of a child.

Şeyh / Sheik, Sheikh, Shaykh: Literal meaning: elder, old man

"In sufism, it generally means a spiritual leader, teacher, guide, master. In the Whirling Prayer Ceremony (*semâ*), the Shaykh symbolizes the presence of Mawlânâ Jalâluddîn Rûmî. In a Mevlevi center (*tekke*), the Shaykh is the highest authority." (1)

Tasavvuf / Tasawwuf: Mystical dimension of Islam

"It is the mystical science of spiritual purification and seeking nearness to God. Its foundation is the daily worship and the guidelines and boundaries of conduct in Islam (sharî`ah), and its branches are the path (tarîqah), mystical knowledge (ma`rîfah), and ultimate truth (Haqîqah)." (1)

Tarîkat / Tariqat, Religious Order, Way: Literal meaning: road, path, way

"The sufi path of spiritual purification and training in mystical disciplines. Its foundation is the daily worship and the guidelines and boundaries of conduct in Islam (sharî`ah). Generally, the more advanced levels are mystical knowledge (ma`rîfah), and ultimate truth (Haqîqah). The word also means one of the traditional lineages of sufism (tasawwuf), which is the mystical dimension of Islam." (1)

Tekke / Dervish Lodge: "A sufi gathering place, usually separate from mosques. A place (also called (*dargâh*) where dervishes would meet and do prayer-chanting (Zikr) and receive spiritual instruction from the teacher." (1)

Tekkes of the Mevlevi tradition are called Mevlevî Houses (*Mevlevîhâne).*

Tennûre / Dervish Dress (1. Wide-Skirted Mevlevi Ritual Gown, 2. Daily Dress): The *service tennûre* is worn during daily activities, like running errands.

The whirling *tennure* is a white ritual gown worn by semazens during the Whirling Prayer Ceremony *(semâ).* Although its appearance is often mistaken for a skirt, it is a wide-skirted gown.

"The white color of this garment is the same color as the burial cloth for all Muslims." (1) As such, within the context of the *semâ* ritual, it symbolizes the shroud of a dervish's nafs (ego) (2).

Another meaning of *ten-nûr-e* -containing the word *nûr* (light)- is "the dress of light," symbolizing the manifestation of *nûr (divine light)* from the whirler.

Zâviye / Mevlevî House, Dervish Lodge: Literal or generic meaning:

Meaning in Turkish Sufism: A kind of dervish center (*tekke*)

In the Mevlevî Order: Among the two kinds of Mevlevî Houses, zâviyes were the smaller type. (2)

Zikir, Zikr / Dhikr: Literal meaning: remembrance, mentioning

In Sufism: Zikir is a form of praying that signifies "remembrance of Allah."

(1) Gamard, Ibrahim, Glossary of Mevlevi Terms and Definitions: http://www.dar-al-Masnavi.org/mevlevi-glossary.html

(2) International Mevlana Foundation Website: http://mevlanafoundation.com/mevlevi_order_en.html

(3) Öke, Mim Kemal, Mevlana Jalaluddin Rumi, and Sufism: A Dervish's Logbook, Sufi Kitap, Istanbul, 2017.

(4) Oxford Dictionary of Islam

(5) Oxford Dictionary of Middle Ages

(6) The Concise Oxford Dictionary of World Religions

(7) Chittick, William, The Heart of Islamic Philosophy: The Quest for Self-Knowledge in the Teachings of Afdal Al-Din Kashani, Oxford University Press, 2001.